# Indo-Roman Trade

DUCKWORTH DEBATES IN ARCHAEOLOGY
Series Editor: Richard Hodges

# Indo-Roman Trade

## FROM POTS TO PEPPER

Roberta Tomber

Maps by Antony Simpson
Illustrations by Penny Copeland

Duckworth

First published in 2008 by
Gerald Duckworth & Co. Ltd.
90-93 Cowcross Street, London EC1M 6BF
Tel: 020 7490 7300
Fax: 020 7490 0080
info@duckworth-publishers.co.uk
www.ducknet.co.uk

A catalogue record for this book is available
from the British Library

ISBN 978 0 7156 3696 1

Typeset by Ray Davies
Printed and bound in Great Britain by
CPI Antony Rowe, Chippenham, Wiltshire

# Contents

For M.L.T. and I.W.T.

# Preface and acknowledgements

This book is the outcome of my long-established interest in Roman trade. Over time this interest has migrated eastward, its centre shifting but with Rome nevertheless exerting an influence. Like exchange within the Roman Empire, contact throughout the Indian Ocean involves diverse geographical settings, but it is a much broader experience, not only physically, but incorporating traders and merchants from outside the Roman world.

My aim here is to interpret these connections by examining the evidence from throughout the Indian Ocean, not limiting myself to one geographical area. The treatment presents topical issues supported by new evidence, particularly from ceramics, that contributes to ongoing research into Indo-Roman trade. However, the subject is complex and can only be presented in a simplified manner; furthermore, it is advancing at tremendous speed. As I write the final pages, excavations are taking place at Pattanam by the Kerala Council for Historical Research and the Archaeological Survey of India, the results from which will enhance and alter the evidence presented here. Already the amphorae collected from Pattanam promise to exceed those from Arikamedu. However, this book provides a starting point for future studies and future debates.

The main research included here was undertaken while holding an AHRC major research grant with David Peacock. My warmest thanks go to him for enabling me to embark on this project in Archaeology at Southampton University and his support throughout my research. Since 2002 I have been based at the British Museum, in Conservation and Scientific Research. This has provided a congenial and dynamic atmosphere and for this I thank my colleagues and particularly David Saunders (Keeper) and Catherine Higgit (Head of Science) and former members of the department, Sheridan Bowman and Ian Freestone.

The initial impetus, and much of the original data, for this book came from my participation in excavations at Berenike (Steve Sidebotham and Willeke Wendrich), Quseir al-Qadim (David Peacock and Lucy Blue), and post-excavation on Aqaba (Tom Parker), and I am grateful to those project directors for facilitating my work on their pottery. The success of my research in India is due to the generosity and hospitality of many individuals, but P.J. Cherian, Sunil Gupta, K. Krishnan, V. Selvakumar and K.P. Shajan have been the connecting thread for a number of trips and their significant input is recorded here with gratitude.

The list of colleagues and friends from whom I have benefited is enormous, from sharing sherds to ideas. It is with pleasure that I thank the Archaeological Survey of India, K.K. Bahn, Anne Benoist, René Cappers, Rob Carter, Caroline Cartwright, Dilip Chakrabarti, John Cooper, Paul Craddock, Peter De Geest, Deccan College Museum, Vishwas Gogte, Kevin Greene, Indian Archaeological Society, Atusha Irani, Shahnaj Jahan, Kalini Khandwalla, Sean Kingsley, Ajit Kumar, Madras University Museum, Andrew Middleton, M.S. Baroda University Museum, Jacke Phillips, David Phillipson, Rukshana Nanji, Paul Nicholson, Pondicherry Museum, Alex Porter, Debraj Pradhan, Shubhra Pramanik, K.P. Rajan, Jennifer Ramsay, P. Ravitchandirane, Margaret Sax, Alexander Sedov, Sushmita Sen, Gautam Sengupta, V. Shinde, St. John Simpson, Carla Sinopoli, Ross Thomas, Alok Tripathi,

Sila Tripathi, S. Vasanthi, Walter Ward, J.-H. Weisshaar, John Peter Wild and Julian Whitewright. I also thank the late Vimala Begley and Peter Francis, whose knowledge and enthusiasm are sorely missed.

Lucy Blue, Catherine Johns and Melvyn Firth helped me enormously throughout the course of writing, and commented on the entire text; to them I owe a special debt. Other friends and colleagues have shared their expertise and also read specific chapters, and I am grateful to them for their comments and time: Shinu Abraham, Niall Finneran, Sunil Gupta, Derek Kennet, Sam Moorhead, Heidrun Schenk and Steve Sidebotham. A number of the pottery figures are based on original drawings by Christine Dijkstra, Gillian Pyke, Graham Reed and Julian Whitewright, whom I thank.

Of course, without Duckworth there would be no book – and it is therefore with great pleasure that I thank Deborah Blake and Richard Hodges for their encouragement and support.

Finally, the diacriticals for Arabic and Indian languages familiar to many scholars have not been used here, because of the diverse ways of implementing them into English.

# List of illustrations

*List of illustrations*

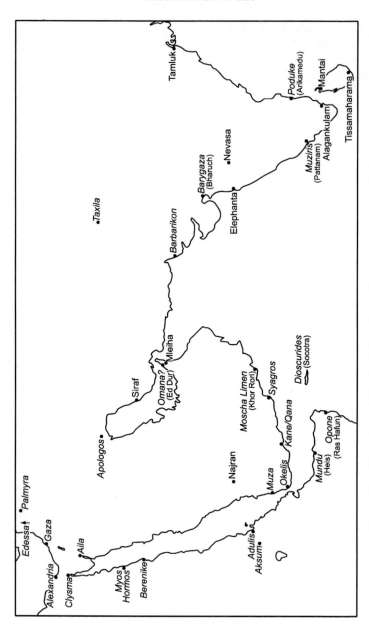

Fig. 1. Map of key sites within the Indian Ocean (for detailed maps see Figs 12, 15-19).

# 1

# Introducing Indo-Roman trade

## Wheeler's discovery of Rome in India

I went up to a covered case and swept a sweaty forearm across the glass. The result might be described as electric. Where there had just previously spread an impermeable layer of dust was now displayed a considerable crust of fragmentary Graeco-Roman amphorae, and amidst them were sherds of red ware of the sort that any student of things classical could readily recognize ... And now here at last in Pondicherry was journey's end; precisely those ancient and dateable fabrics in a context which in southern India gave them and their associations a new meaning to us in time and space. They opened in fact a new field in the broad world of comparative archaeology (Wheeler 1976: 41).

Thus was Sir Mortimer Wheeler inspired to excavate at Arikamedu between April and June 1945. And it is the site at Arikamedu, and Wheeler's interpretation of the site, that has since dominated our perception of Indo-Roman trade. Wheeler repeatedly disseminated his view in such classics as *Rome Beyond the Imperial Frontiers* (1954b), *Archaeology from the Earth* (1954a), *Still Digging* (1955) and *My Archaeological Mission to India and Pakistan* (1976). These publications reinforced an existing orthodoxy of Indo-Roman trade clearly set out by E.H. Warmington, as being Roman controlled (1928: 1-2). In this schema, Arikamedu was a foreign city colonised by

13

Roman traders during the first and second centuries AD (Wheeler 1951: 354-8). While Arikamedu has held a unique place in Indo-Roman trade, because of its concentration of Roman artefacts (Wheeler found 116 sherds of amphorae and 38 of *terra sigillata*), it has also maintained this position because of the influence of Wheeler. These two factors have together resulted in Arikamedu having a 'stranglehold on Indian historical writing' (Ray 1998: 49), as well as on Early Historic chronology (Ravitchandrane 2007).

Wheeler's framework obviously owes much to his time and place, being unashamedly a member of the British Empire. From his arrival as Director General of the Archaeological Survey of India, one of Wheeler's undertakings was to catalogue the Roman coins there. In addition, he established a pottery typology for local pottery dated in reference to Roman ceramic type-fossils, still relied upon throughout South India. Both the coins and pottery were published in the Arikamedu report in *Ancient India* (Wheeler et al. 1946). Equally resilient is his interpretive model of terminal and transit trade. Transit involved Indian centres that served as entrepots between the West and East and where Western finds were relatively rare; terminal referred to centres where local products were in demand in exchange for Western goods (Wheeler 1951: 352-4).

A further legacy of Wheeler was teaching young Indian scholars at the Taxila Training School, inspiring a generation who remained committed to the study of Indo-Roman trade. Despite active scholarship in India, Wheeler's vision of Indo-Roman trade went essentially unchallenged until the re-excavation of Arikamedu in the late 1980s by Begley (et al. 1996, 2004). Begley's choice of Arikamedu is in itself a potent reminder of its role as the principal Indian site for Indo-Roman trade.

# 1. Introducing Indo-Roman trade

## Contextualising Indo-Roman trade (Fig. 1)

Indo-Roman trade comprises a small episode within the much broader history of Indian Ocean activity. This interaction was characterised not only by the exchange of goods, but also culture, such as shared language. The convergence of textual and archaeological evidence during the Classical period makes it an especially rich field. From the fifth millennium BC, small networks operated within the larger realm, exploiting the two main arteries of the Arabian/Persian Gulf (hereafter the Gulf) and the Red Sea (Salles 1998: 58, 66). Bronze Age trade between north-west India and the Gulf (Ratnagar 2006) and Old Kingdom links between Egypt and East Africa (Kitchen 2004) are but two examples. Under the Seleucids (312-60 BC), during the Hellenistic period, Indian trade reached the Eastern Mediterranean via the Gulf, following the Euphrates and eventually overland to Antioch or Gaza (Salles 1998: 58). During the Roman period the Red Sea became more active than previously. Although not continuous, contacts intensified from their beginning, through European expansion and into the modern day.

The inspiration for Indo-Roman trade can be traced to Alexander, whose achievements loomed large in the Roman mind. His Indian campaign of 327 BC, from which Megathenes and Eratosthenes reported the wonders of the East, continued to engage the Roman imagination (Whittaker 1998: 11, 15). Augustus modelled himself after Alexander and even 300 years later Trajan reportedly said 'I should certainly have crossed over to the Indi, too, if I were still young' (Dio Cassius *History* 68.29). The Roman appetite for goods from India was fuelled by this idea of India (Parker 2002: 55).

More tangibly, Indo-Roman trade was concerned with the acquisition of natural resources and manufactured products that could be obtained from the East. Conventionally these items have been considered luxury goods. Gibbons (1993: 64), for example, referred to Rome's trade with the East as 'splendid but trifling' (McPherson 1995: 78). There are numerous textual allusions to the financial and moral decadence arising from the consumption of luxury goods. First-century AD examples include Trimalchio's extravagant dinner party described by Petronius in the *Satyricon* (Parker 2002: 58) and senatorial debates reported on by Tacitus (De Romanis 1997b: 90, 123-8).

Gems, silks and ostentatious consumption represent the luxury end of the market. But more and more it has been demonstrated that many objects of trade – including pepper and aromatics – became necessities for the Roman way of life, required for medicinal and religious purposes (Sidebotham 1986: 15; McPherson 1995: 79-82). Even the culinary use of spices gradually became more widespread. Changes in textual references reflect this: in 13 BC Horace described pepper as being wrapped in small packets, but by the mid-first century AD, Apicius' recipes use generous amounts regularly (Whittaker 2004: 171-2). Essentials or not, these goods would not have been equally available to all segments of society. As a comparison, a Roman pound of pepper cost 32 times more than a pound of bread. Nevertheless, it was pepper, other spices and aromatics that drove the trade between East and West, so much so that in India black pepper was sometimes known as '*yavanapriya*' (loved by the foreigner) (De Romanis 1997b: 100). The Indians too had a taste for pepper and throughout the country it was desired (Achaya 1994: 47). Yet pepper was an inexpensive commodity in India, so it could be exported for large profits (Thapar 1997: 27).

## Reassessing Indo-Roman trade

Since Wheeler's time new methods have been developed by which to locate, excavate and record sites. As an example, the ancient ports of Myos Hormos in Egypt (Peacock 1993) and

## 1. Introducing Indo-Roman trade

Muziris in south-west India (Shajan et al. 2004) have been located. The excavation of these and other sites has transformed our perception of Indo-Roman trade. Equally, rigorous collection strategies and analytical techniques have allowed more refined sourcing of finds, especially pottery (Tomber 2007b) and botanical remains (Cappers 2006) that inform on items exchanged and, indirectly, on their routes. Moreover, the complexity of interaction and the different mechanisms involved, from barter to commercial exchange subsumed within trade, is recognised through a more sophisticated theoretical basis (Ray 1995b).

It is therefore timely to re-evaluate Indo-Roman trade by asking questions such as:

What goods were exchanged and what others travelled alongside?
Who controlled the trade?
Who conducted the trade?
Where did the traders live?
What routes were followed and how do artefacts inform on these routes?
What was the duration and extent of trade through time?

The geographical setting for these questions reaches far beyond Roman and Indian ports. The Roman Red Sea, East Africa, the Gulf, South Arabia and India can be conceived as a series of interlocking regions, each with its own complex history, culture, social and political systems. The boundaries set for this study were largely determined by key sites – particularly coastal ones – that imported foreign goods and exported local products. Through them the multi-cultural nature of the ancient world, in terms of both people and commodities, is emphasised.

Traditionally Indo-Roman trade has been placed between

the reigns of Augustus and Marcus Aurelius, after which not only is it thought to have reduced, but to have been conducted primarily through non-Roman middlemen. Although the Red Sea ports were active before this time, it was with the annexation of Egypt by Augustus in 30 BC that the systematic exploitation of trade routes for primarily economic purposes commenced. This relied upon an understanding of the monsoon cycles. Although long harnessed by Indians, Arabs and Persians, and known by the Greeks from the time of Alexander, they were not systematically exploited by the Romans until the Augustan era (Tchernia 1997b: 250-61). Thus in this volume the timeframe opens with Augustus. It continues to the early or mid-seventh century and highlights new evidence pertaining to the fourth century and beyond.

It was the pottery especially that led Wheeler to Arikamedu and so too it is new pottery evidence that has provided the impetus for this review of Indo-Roman trade. Of course, pottery alone is not sufficient to achieve a balanced picture of activity in the Indian Ocean, and in Chapter 2 we will discuss the different types of material and textual evidence available. Chapters 3-5 take us on the journey from the Red Sea to the East. A final chapter integrates the evidence from these different regions to achieve an overview of their interactions through time, thus departing from Wheeler's more colonial vision.

# 2

# Charting exchange through texts and objects

Our knowledge of ancient long-distance trade is made visible through many classes of evidence, from durable materials such as pottery and stone, to more fragile organic finds such as archaeobotanical and faunal remains and textiles. Other materials, such as metals, survive well but were often recycled in antiquity, thus, in terms of original typology and chronology, blurring the archaeological record. In this chapter we focus on the potential of coins, pottery and archaeobotany, all of which have contributed substantially to our understanding of Indian Ocean commerce. Written documents provide another dimension to our narrative, frequently on matters otherwise invisible from the sites. Of the different categories of evidence available for tracing ancient trade, each has its own particular strengths and weaknesses and it is only by combining this evidence and interpreting it in context that we begin to build up a balanced picture of the past (Wendrich et al. 2003).

## Texts or documents and inscriptions

By its explicit nature the written word is often taken at face value and treated as fact, but like any other type of evidence it needs to be critically evaluated. It is appropriate to begin with these sources for, until recently, they formed the main evidence for Indo-Roman trade, brought together in such central works as Warmington (1928) and Raschke (1978). All the societies directly involved in the Indo-Roman trade network were literate, but we concentrate on Classical and Indian documents, in this section drawing on examples that illustrate the range of writers and their subjects.

## Greek and Latin writings

For the classical period surviving texts may be either official or private and cover a range of subjects and genres from literary to legal. A range of caveats including the bias of the writer and inaccuracies, resulting either from lack of knowledge or the desire to idealise a situation as intentional propaganda, must be borne in mind. Additionally, many of these writings are in accepted shorthand that was implicitly understood in Antiquity but can be problematic to interpret now. Much of their value therefore relates to what can be inferred, rather than what is explicitly stated. Practical difficulties also exist as the documents available to us today are normally copies of copies, transcribed during Antiquity or later, with errors creeping in at every stage of the process.

Nevertheless, documents provide a historical backdrop and add a personal dimension that is frequently absent from other classes of evidence. In this respect the *Periplus Maris Erythraei* is unique. The voice here is that of a Greco-Egyptian merchant living in Alexandria who, in 66 short sections, described the waters and ports from the Red Sea to India, itemising the goods coming in and out of these ports and the people encountered at each. It is a practical guide aimed at merchants. The writer appears to have had firsthand knowledge of many of these places. His is the most detailed written account of the sea journey and archaeologists eagerly dissect it for clues to locate ports not yet known on the ground. The author had wide-ranging interests and the main strengths of the *Periplus* are vivid descriptions, but he didn't explicitly analyse the relationships between different areas and trading partners.

The accuracy of the *Periplus* is being increasingly upheld for locating ancient sites and for descriptions of distances, in both *stadia* (each 185 metres) and the travel time between them. It has been enormously informative in locating sites such as Myos Hormos (Peacock 1993) and Adulis (Peacock & Blue 2007). In terms of the flow of objects, it refers to many items – such as sesame oil and ghee – that are no longer visible in the archaeological record and therefore supplements our knowledge. However, many items that travelled are not mentioned in the *Periplus*. Despite the strict regulation of Oriental commerce to ensure that the 25% state tax levied on imports was collected (Sidebotham 1986: 177), some contraband would have slipped through, just as some goods would have been illegally sold off on their way to the ports.

The earliest preserved manuscript of the *Periplus Maris Erythraei* dates to the early tenth century and different English translations illustrate the scope for alternative interpretations of the text (Schoff 1912; Huntingford 1980). Casson's 1989 commentary is relied upon here; as the most recent it forms part of an ongoing analysis of this rich text.

The date of the text has been the subject of longstanding debate, favouring a period between the first and mid-third centuries AD. However, a mid-first century timeframe is confirmed obliquely through the political geography. *PME* 19 refers to Malichus, king of the Nabataeans, and while there was more than one king Malichus this one appears to be Malichus II who ruled between AD 40 and 70 (Casson 1989: 7). Although Malichus is the most securely dated, other historical figures occur. For instance a reference in *PME* 41 to Manbanos is taken to be a Hellenisation of the Saka ruler Nahapana (ibid.: 47, 197-8). His conventional reign has been understood as AD 119-124, but more recently one beginning in either AD 48 or 52 has been suggested (Jha & Rajgor 1992: 5; Turner & Cribb 1996).

Other Early Roman authors provide more limited glimpses into Indian Ocean trade, many differing from the writer of the *Periplus* by being named historical figures rather than anonymous. As a result their texts are more easily dated, and more is known about their approach and potential biases. Among the more important of these is Pliny the Elder (AD 23-79). Prolific in his output, his only surviving text is the *Natural History* (*NH*), a 37-book Latin encyclopaedia. Completed in AD 77, it was published after his death, which famously resulted from his inhalation of the fumes of Vesuvius. That he specially visited Vesuvius to observe its eruption speaks well for his scientific method, and with 100 collaborators he included 20,000 facts (*NH* Preface: 13). However, some of this information was secondary and he failed to reconcile conflicting accounts; thus the volume is uneven in its reliability. In the present context, Book 6.101-6 is pertinent in describing the lands involved in Indian Ocean commerce, including the voyage from the Red Sea to India, and Books 12-13 the natural products of the region. Pliny's purpose differs from that of the author of the *Periplus* for he takes a moralising tone and bemoans the effect of Eastern trade on Roman society (Thapar 1997: 15-16; Tchernia 1997b: 252).

Many other ancient writers also based their texts on secondary information. For instance, the Armenian Strabo (*c.* 64/3 BC-AD 23) wrote a 17-book *Geography* in Greek around the early decades of the first century. Although Strabo travelled in Egypt, Yemen and Ethiopia, many of his accounts are derived from earlier writers, including Agatharchides of Cnidus, who wrote *On the Erythraean Sea* shortly before 100 BC and in turn had absorbed the work of earlier writers (Burstein 1989: 13, 22, 29-33). The historians of Alexander the Great, Mark Antony and Augustus also provided source material for Strabo.

## 2. Charting exchange through texts and objects

Less written evidence is available for the Late Roman period, an imbalance that has reinforced the consensus that the Early Roman period was the peak of Indo-Roman trade. There are no documents for the late period equivalent to the *Periplus*, but the illustrated *Christian Topography* comes the closest. Like the *Periplus* it was penned by an Alexandrian merchant, probably importing spices, whose nickname Cosmas *Indicopleustes* (Indian traveller) dates to the eleventh century. But here the two diverge: Cosmas' main interest was theological, rather than geographical, and his world view reflects his affiliation with Nestorian Christianity, whereas the *Periplus* mentions religion only once (Casson 1989: 10). Despite this emphasis Cosmas described, with what is considered great accuracy, his travels to the Mediterranean, the Nile Valley, Sinai, Palestine, the Persian Gulf, Ethiopia, Eritrea and even Socotra. He appears to have had only second-hand knowledge of India and Sri Lanka. Of the eastern coast of Somalia, and further south, he had none (Wolska-Conus 1968: 16-17). As with the *Periplus*, the date of *Christian Topography* is most clearly derived through historical persons and events. Book 2.56 states it was written about 25 years after the Aksumite expedition to Arabia AD 523-5 (Wolska-Conus 1968: 16-17, 369, otherwise cited as AD 524-5), placing it *c.* AD 548-50, although it was probably worked on from at least AD 535 (McCrindle 1897: x-xi). Cosmas probably wrote the book in retirement in an Egyptian monastery.

The spread of Christianity to the East was a matter of central interest to many Christian writers, including Rufinus (*c.* 345-410) and Athanasius (*c.* 295-373). However, there are difficulties in interpreting these texts, since India may refer to modern India, Ethiopia or South Arabia, depending on the writer (Mayerson 1993). Aksum in Ethiopia has been called part of Inner India, Innermost India or Further India.

Mayerson concludes that, with the exception of Cosmas, Hellenistic and Early Roman writers generally had a more accurate perception of India than the Byzantine ones. Salles, on the other hand, sees geographical terminology not merely as Mayerson's 'confusion of Indias', but reflecting changes in mental maps due to 'geo-political circumstances' (1998: 67).

Official sources include the Alexandrian Tariff, which was codified under Marcus Aurelius (AD 176-180) and later included in Justinian's *Digest* (AD 533). Listing those spices subject to the 25% import duty, it included white and long pepper, but not black (Miller 1969: 25, 279-80; see below).

In a different category are non-literary texts found in the Eastern Desert of Egypt occurring as both papyri and *ostraca* – writing on pot sherds – that are concerned with trade within and beyond the region. Although rare elsewhere in the Roman Empire, *ostraca* are common in the Eastern Desert because of preservation conditions. One group of 90 linked *ostraca* from Coptos was published by Sir Flinders Petrie. Known as the Nicanor archive, it comprises receipts for a family shipping firm operating between Coptos, on the Nile, and the Red Sea ports of Berenike and Myos Hormos between 6 BC and AD 68/69; it lists foodstuffs interpreted as provisions for both the ports and the overseas journey, and as items of trade (Fuks 1951; Bagnall et al. 2000: 8).

More recently a group of *ostraca* originating from a customs house was excavated from a rubbish dump at Berenike with two precisely dated *ostraca:* 6 August 33 and 20 September 61. The later one is a receipt similar to those in the Nicanor archive and written in Coptos (Bagnall et al. 2000: 7). The other *ostraca* and finds suggest that, overall, the rubbish was accumulated between *c.* 40/5 and 70/5 AD. Most of these Berenike *ostraca* are passes for the Berenike customs station, enabling the bearer to enter with itemised goods, most commonly wine, for both export and provisions (ibid.: 8).

## 2. Charting exchange through texts and objects

By their very quantity, groups of related *ostraca* tend to be more informative in terms of their historical context than when occurring singly. However, as the archive of named persons involved in trade in the Eastern Desert expands even a single *ostracon* can be instructive. For example, a letter from Myos Hormos mentioned Peteasmephis, a rare name that occurred in the Nicanor archive as one of Nicanor's agents at Myos Hormos and Berenike in AD 6 (Van Rengen 2003: 43; Bagnall et al. 2000: 25).

Another document, this time written on papyrus, is a legal text known as the 'Muziris papyrus'. Purchased in 1980 by the Austrian National Library, its provenance is unknown, but Rathbone (2001) considers it to come from Oxyrhynchus in the Fayum, a site renowned for the vast quantities of papyri recovered by Grenfell and Hunt from the last years of the nineteenth century. The text covers both sides of the papyrus; both concern aspects of Oriental trade and date to the mid-second century, although the writing is in different hands. Neither is complete, but the front or *recto* is a supplement to a maritime loan contract for a journey between Alexandria and Muziris, providing detailed instructions for transporting goods from the Red Sea to Alexandria. The back, or *verso*, itemises the value of a ship's cargo of Gangetic nard (an aromatic plant used to make ointment or perfume), ivory and textiles, after the 25% tax was deducted. Why the loan required a supplement, whether it involved merchants, ship owners or financiers, whether the texts were written in Alexandria, at a Red Sea site or at Muziris, have all been debated (Casson 1986; Rathbone 2001).

Epigraphic evidence is a related but separate category of writing on objects and includes inscriptions, coins and graffiti. The first two, especially, can be formulaic and depend on a thorough knowledge of these sub-disciplines. Graffiti comprise a much more opportunistic category. On pottery, for instance, they often provide information on who used the vessel and where, and in the Eastern Desert they provide insights into their ethnicity. On a larger scale, Nabataean cave inscriptions and graffiti can be found throughout the Eastern Desert (Sidebotham 1986: 94).

## Indian texts

Indian texts come from an entirely different tradition from the Roman ones cited above. For South India, Tamil poems collected into thematic anthologies known as the *Sangam* literature are informative and frequently quoted (Champakalakshmi 2006: 175-80). Many are epic or heroic, revolving around raids and plunders; economic matters are secondary to the main intention of the poems. Importantly, they demonstrate a special interest in the environment and man's relationship to it through the description of eco-zones or '*tinai*' (Champakalakshmi 2006: 177; Gurukkal 1995).

The *Sangam* poems were composed over a long period by persons of varying occupation (e.g. merchants, potters and carpenters) as well as varying social groups (e.g. princes, chieftains and peasants) and, like the Classical documents, they were recopied over time. A general consensus of their date ranges between 300 BC and AD 300 (e.g. Morrison 2002: 33). Within the *Sangam* corpus the poems are divided into eight anthologies, for which there is some relative dating. The *Akananuru* and the *Purananuru*, which mention Muziris (Muchiri), are thought to be among the earliest, while the somewhat later *Pattinappalai* describes Kaveripattinam on the east coast (Champakalakshmi 2006: 179-80; Zvelebil 1973: 42-3). Post-*Sangam* Tamil epics are also relevant, including the *Cilappatikaram*, which is dated into the fifth century (Zvelebil 1974: 132). Seland has counted *c.* 50 references to trade and 10 to *yavanas* in the Tamil literature –

insignificant numbers in more than 2,000 poems (2006: 45, 2007b: 71).

The relationship between the *tinai* provides valuable information on the dynamics of interregional or internal exchange in subsistence goods. *Yavanas*, an umbrella term that includes foreigners of diverse origin, were important in facilitating external trade, but they also assumed other roles. The term originates in Sanskrit, and probably derives from the Prakrit term *yona*, in turn derived from Ionia in Achaemenid inscriptions (Thapar 2002: 159-60). Ray suggests that around the turn of the Christian era in the north-west and west, the term *yavana* referred to Greeks and Indo-Greeks, while in peninsular India and in the *Sangam* primarily to visitors from the Roman East concerned with trade (1995c). By the fourth century Arabs and West Asians were also subsumed within the term. *Yavanas* are mentioned in cave inscriptions of the western Deccan as donors to the local Buddhist establishments. Some *yavana* names even suggest conversion to Buddhism, which may have been genuine but also would have advanced their status among the local trading networks (Thapar 1997: 34-5). In contrast to other donors, *yavanas* do not name their occupation – possibly because they were exclusively traders (Ray 1985: 28; 1995: 80-1, citing Dehejia 1972). The *Sangam* hints that by the second century the *yavanas* had established settlements and were involved in more diverse occupations, including royal guards and skilled craftsmen (Champakalakshmi 2006: 109). De Romanis has suggested that the *yavana* guards arrived in India as archers, protecting Western ships from pirates (1997b: 104).

For the north, the document that has most relevance is the Sanskrit *Arthashastra*. This is an idealised text on government, describing the internal organisation of the state and its relationship with external states (Chande 1998: 10). The original is thought to be from the time of Chandragupta

27

(early fourth century BC ), but the present document belongs to around the third century AD. Whether or what parts of it are actually Mauryan is therefore controversial (Thapar 2002: 184-5). The *Arthashastra* is of limited value since it is a theoretical text and its date cannot be accurately determined. It does, however, describe aspects of production and exchange facilitated through the *shreni* (guilds) and *vanij* (merchants) (ibid.: 248-51).

## *Interfacing documents*

Although politically India was not a Roman province, it sometimes appears as such on lists, and Emperors from Augustus to the fourth century AD considered Indians their subjects (Whittaker 1998: 1-5). Classical and Indian writings reveal their attitudes towards each other. For the Romans, both ideas and attitudes stem from Alexander, in part because of the desire to emulate him. Tales of the fantastic, originating during Alexander's time, such as dragons, griffins and monsters with enormous bodies (Jerome *Letters* 125.3; Parker 2002: 47; see also Parker 2008) or rivers of wine, honey and oil (Dio Chrysostom *Discourses* 35.18-24) reinforced the Roman notion of the fantastic East. Thus exoticism was added to the opposition, alterity or 'otherness' of Indians, as eloquently discussed by Whitaker. Romans of higher social standing were more likely to cling to these beliefs, perpetuating a view of 'barbarian Orientalism', while traders and travellers could draw on direct experience (Whittaker 1998: 5-7, 11-19).

Indian attitudes to *yavanas* were uneven between different regions, with Buddhist texts most favourable. Even within the corpus of Tamil poems some ambiguity exists: for example the *yavanas* were valued for the things they brought, such as fragrant wine (Champakalakshmi 2006: 109: Thapar 1997: 37-8), yet as traders they were referred to as 'the uncivilised

*Yavanas* of harsh speech' (*Patirruppattu* 2, trans. Zvelebil 1956: 404). While seemingly derogatory, as bodyguards they possessed some attributes that made them particularly suitable for their task: 'the hard-eyed *Yavanas* of terrible appearance, whose body is of strong joints ...' (*Mullaippattu* 59-61, trans. Zvebil ibid.)

## Maps

Maps frequently had a direct link with texts and provide a visual representation of how the ancients conceptualised their world and viewed themselves in relation to others. Claudius Ptolemy (*c.* AD 100-170) – an Alexandria-based Egyptian, writing in Greek, devised an earth-centred model of the universe. He provided longitude and latitude, ranging between Ireland and Cattigara (Vietnam), incorporating information from the work of Marinus of Tyre (*c.* AD 100). Ptolemy's co-ordinates were intended for the production of a world map and 26 regional ones as part of his eight-book, mid-second-century *Geography*. Numerous copies of Ptolemy's maps exist, for they were relied upon until they were improved during the Age of Exploration. Unfortunately Ptolemy underestimated the circumference of the earth, thus miscalculating the distances between any two places, and his maps were increasingly distorted as he moved east. As a result, the Mediterranean Sea and Gulf were elongated, India and Southeast Asia were foreshortened and Sri Lanka was approximately 14 times greater than its actual size (Shasri 2000: xxi). Despite these errors, Ptolemy was knowledgeable about the East. His descriptions of India differed from those of Pliny and the *Periplus* and, like the *Sangam* poetry, may well reflect the evolution in trading patterns and emporia between the first and second centuries (Casson 1995; Groom 1994: 202). Seland and others argue that Ptolemy's topography was reworked later and represents the situation between the Late Roman period and the eleventh century (2007b: 73-4). However, as we shall see, the correspondence between Ptolemy and Indian texts and Roman coin distribution in India suggests otherwise.

A graphic document that depicts Roman conceptions of the East is the *Tabula Peutingeriana.* It belongs to a distinct type of road map or *itinerarium pictum* (painted itinerary) and was compiled from itineraries (lists of places and the distances between them on established routes) (Dilke 1985: 112). Unlike the tradition of *periploi*, which were intended for commercial or official travel, *tabulae* served the needs of individuals who had to travel beyond their local area (Salway 2001: 59).

The original Peutinger Table was drawn around the mid-fourth century AD and is preserved as a medieval copy (ibid.: 30-1). It incorporates the entire world as known by the Romans, including India and the Far East. An architectural feature pictured in South India has frequently been identified as a Temple of Augustus at Muziris and by implication used to emphasise the importance of Roman culture in the area. Metzler has recently suggested that a Roman temple could have been established by local chieftains as a diplomatic gesture (Ray 1998: 66, citing Metzler 1989). It is equally plausible that a religious structure existed on the spot, which the Romans merely represented as a monument familiar to them (Ray ibid.).

## Coins (Fig. 2)

What may well be the most frequent citation on Indo-Roman trade involves coinage. Of the Red Sea route, Pliny wrote:

> ... in no year does India absorb less than fifty million *sesterces* of our empire's wealth, sending back merchan-

dise to be sold with us at a hundred times its prime cost
(*NH* 12.101).

Whether the evidence on the ground supports such
extravagant claims is another matter. Burnett (1998: 179) and
De Romanis (1997b: 119-22) are in the minority in thinking
that Pliny's statistics are realistic (contra Sidebotham 1986:
36-9; Rathbone 2001: 47-9). Certainly the 50,000,000 HS
quoted by Pliny is not a particularly large amount, given that
the personal wealth of some senators was six times this (De
Romanis 1997b: 121).

Without doubt coins form a significant data resource and
gold and silver issues particularly have received much
attention. Elliott provided the first attempt at a comprehensive
survey in 1844; Wheeler catalogued 68 coin find spots (1951:
375-80). More recently *c.* 75 find spots comprising more than
6,000 *denarii* (silver) and 800 *aurei* (gold) of the first to third
centuries were published by Turner in *Roman Coins in India*
(1989; Ray 1995c: 86). Suresh's recent study has added further
examples and MacDowall's forthcoming gazetteer will double
the number of entries since Wheeler (Suresh 2004: 160-77;
MacDowall 1998: 81). The combined effort of over a hundred
years of scholarship means that the identifications and
distribution of coins are reliable, but their interpretation
remains controversial.

Most of the Roman coins in India – over 70% of the silver and
90% of the gold – occurred as hoards in the south, especially the
south-west (Meyer 2007: 61). Most are Julio-Claudian in date,
although rare Republican coins are present, frequently found
with later issues up to Hadrian (MacDowall 1998: 89).

Turner identified three main hoard types among the
precious metals (1989: 42-3). The accuracy of their reportage is
variable and the largest comprises just over 1,500 coins.
Turner's first hoard type, of early Julio-Claudian coins (mostly

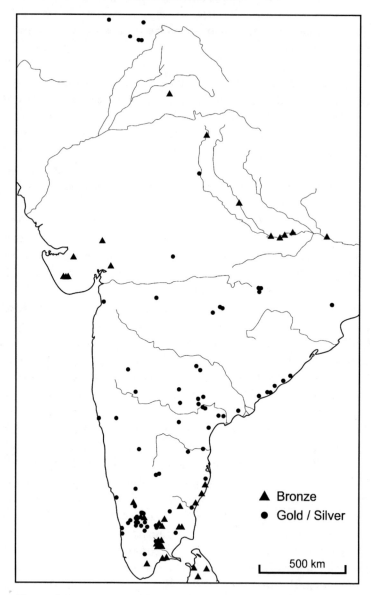

Fig. 2. Schematic map of Roman coins in India and Sri Lanka (after Berghaus 1991: 121; MacDowall 1998: fig. 9 and Turner 1989: map 1).

Augustus and Tiberius), tend to be *denarii*, of a limited number
of issues and in fairly good condition. Turner thought these
were selected by Indians and buried near to the centre of trade.
The second hoard type, of later Julio-Claudian coins (mostly
Tiberius and Claudius), is normally formed of *aurei*. These
comprise fewer coins, but are of a larger number of types and
more widespread (ibid.: 24, 27). Unlike the *denarii* they are in
a worn condition. A third hoard type, of post-Julio-Claudian
coins often with earlier ones, consists of *aurei*. Second-century
*aurei* are generally in excellent condition (ibid.: 42). After a
lacuna in the third century, a fourth hoard type not discussed
in full by Turner is the gold *solidi*, mostly of the fourth and fifth
centuries with occasional later ones extending into the sixth
and even early seventh century (MacDowall 1998: 81; Meyer
2007: 60).

Two regions had particularly dense concentrations of
hoards. The first, Coimbatore, is located between the west and
east coasts in a region associated with gems, a lucrative trade
item. These hoards are primarily Julio-Claudian in date
(Turner 1989: 5). The Krishna River in Andhra Pradesh forms
the second group; in contrast these are post-Julio-Claudian,
mostly second century (ibid.: 5-6). The situation in northern
India was radically different, for Roman coin finds comprise
less than a quarter of those found in South India (Thapar 2002:
253). They tend to occur individually or in small numbers and
are mostly post-Julio-Claudian.

Bronze coinage has received considerably less attention;
Wheeler emphasised the lack of first- and second-century
denominations (1954b: 139). MacDowall alludes to a few finds
and with his additions, bronze coinage was present in India
from the Early Empire into the fifth century (1998: 91). They
occur particularly along the Yamuna and Ganges, in Gujarat,
and in South India along the Coromandel Coast, near the
Palghat Gap and at Karur and Madurai (ibid.: 91-2, fig. 9).

Krishnamurthy has published a selection of nearly 4,500, mostly from the river beds of Karur, dating between the mid-fourth and fifth centuries (2007: 19, 91).

At least some bronze coinage may have circulated, but interpretation of the precious coinage is more complex, and why and when it arrived in India is controversial. Warmington's view, that a Roman currency may have been established in South India, has never gained support (1928: 278). Instead Wheeler established the orthodoxy for silver and gold coins, that they were bullion for exchange by weight rather than for monetary circulation (1954b: 137-45). He based his argument largely on the lack of local coinage in precious metal, although this was somewhat overstated (Lal Gupta 1991: 125).

It is not possible to generalise entirely about the indigenous coin situation in India as there were important differences between the north and west, compared with more marginal areas (Thapar 2002: 253). Furthermore, a distinction must be made between the use of precious and semi-precious metals. Indigenous coinage in base metals was common during the Early Historic period, in precious metals much less so, but nevertheless a coin culture did exist. In South India silver punch-marked coins existed and are occasionally found in hoards with Roman ones. This could suggest that Roman coins were used as currency, as might the existence of sparse low-value local coins in imitation of Roman ones (ibid.; Lal Gupta 1991: 125.). Additionally, punch-marked coins are found alongside Roman coins and coin moulds at Kondapur. Other examples of precious metal coins are from the north and include silver Satavahana (Ray 1985: 30-1) and Kshatrapa ones that were variable in quality (Turner 1989: 23). Exceptionally, the silver coins of the Kshatrapa ruler Nahapana are of such fine quality that it has been suggested they were produced by melting down *denarii* (Turner & Cribb 1996: 312). As Thapar has pointed out, coinage is unlikely to have been systematically reused, since the Classical sources do not mention it (2002: 252-3). A gold coin very similar to the *aureus* was struck by the Kushanas and, again, the suggestion is put forth that they were made from restruck *aurei* (Wheeler 1954b: 142). Alternatively, the Kushanas may have struck their own coins this way so they would be legal tender in areas familiar with Roman currency (Thapar 2002: 253).

References to Roman coinage in the *Periplus* reinforce the varying roles that money played in different parts of India. From these texts, Casson infers that coinage was used for barter at Barygaza (*PME* 49) and as currency at Barbarikon (*PME* 39) and in Tamil country (*PME* 56) (Casson 1989: 30-1; Ray 1991: 60). The implication is that although Barygaza and Barbarikon were both in coin using areas, the nature of transactions differed. In the mid-second century Pausanias (*Laconia* 3.12.3-4) wrote 'Those who sail to India say that the natives give other merchandise in exchange for Greek cargoes, knowing nothing about coinage, and that though they have plenty of gold and of bronze.' Whittaker interprets this not as the state of affairs, but lack of information on the part of Pausanias (2004: 173). Gurukkal is adamant that Roman coins did not circulate in South India 'since the very nature of their modes of exchange precluded it' (1995: 250). It is likely that the type or scale of the transaction was more important than geographical or chronological considerations. The Indian *Jatakas* (Buddhist texts) speak of a combination of monetary transactions and barter in the economy depending on the scale, and a similar situation may have existed for external trade as well (Ray 1985: 28); another important distinction would have existed between the use of precious and non-precious coins.

At present there is agreement that precious coins were generally used for bullion. Whether they can be used to date and chart the relative intensity of trade with India is more controversial. Like Wheeler (1954b: 141), Turner applied the coin dates at face value. This led her to propose that trade was most intense during the early first century; furthermore she identified revivals of trade by small peaks under Antoninus Pius and Septimius Severus (1989: 11, 42-3).

On the basis of composition, wear and comparison with hoards in the Empire, MacDowall argues forcibly that the coins reached India only after currency reforms, when they no longer circulated in the Empire (1998). Most of the Julio-Claudian *denarii* in India date before AD 54/5, correlating with a minor reduction in silver purity by Nero; *aurei* date from before the better known reform of AD 64 (MacDowall 1998: 83, 89). One theory is that certain issues of reliable weight were recognised by Indian traders and were specially selected for trade with India (ibid.: 89; Burnett 1998: 181). In this model most pre-AD 64 Julio-Claudian precious coins were imported to India during the Flavian period and slightly later (MacDowall 1998: 94; Burnett 1998: 184-5); post-AD 64 *aurei* during the mid- and later second century and Republican *denarii* during the first half of the second century (MacDowall ibid.). This is problematic as it leaves no extant coinage representing trade between the times of Augustus and Nero and therefore it is likely that some of the coins travelled nearer their face date. Suresh has also raised this possibility, particularly in reference to Republican coins (2004: 29; Tchernia 1997b: 265). For the later periods, from the second century onwards, it is possible that coinage arrived while still current in the Empire (Burnett 1998: 185). Thus the concentration of second-century coins in Andhra Pradesh supports the apparent intensification of east coast activity during that period.

Defacement and imitation of Roman coinage also have relevance to coin usage in India (Berghaus 1991: 111-12). Although not common, defacement of the Imperial portrait is considered a means by which to remove coinage from circulation (either in India or to prevent its return to the West) (e.g. Turner 1989: 34; Wheeler 1954b: 142). Piercing the coin for hanging, presumably for decorative purposes, was another method of defacement.

Two types of imitations have been identified in India. First are counterfeits, many of them very convincing and probably made both in the Roman world and in India (Turner 1989: 37-40). Another category is Indian *bullae*, moulded discs of ceramic or lead each with a perforated projection on top, that sometimes imitate Roman coinage (Ghosh 1989: 177-8). *Bullae* were fairly common, particularly in the north and Deccan, and it might be argued that this geographic concentration reflects a greater familiarity with coinage.

The smaller number of coin hoards in the north than in the south may reflect its more monetarised economy, with coins reused in the north. Meyer has suggested that the presence of hoards in South India may reflect the political instability between the Chola, Chera and Pandya tribes, so that once buried it was more difficult to return and recover hoards (2007: 62). Other uses of coins and explanations for hoards have been raised. Champakalakshmi has suggested that in South India coins were used as gift exchange between Tamil chiefs and ruling families (2006: 110). Another related possibility is that the concentration of Roman coinage in Coimbatore represents internal transactions among Indians (De Romanis 1997b: 98, n. 79).

Despite unresolved issues regarding the function and date of the exportation of coins to India, their potential as the most precisely identified and largest single category of Roman finds in India makes them essential for interpreting trade. Although overshadowed by Roman ones, other foreign coins – such as Aksumite, Indian and Sasanian ones – circulated in the Indian Ocean and are mentioned in subsequent chapters.

## Pottery

Pottery is only occasionally mentioned in Classical documents and then normally as a container for foodstuffs. Nevertheless it was sometimes a trade item in its own right, or at other times travelled as a personal possession or gift. Research throughout the Indian Ocean has demonstrated that pottery of diverse function and origin was widely distributed. After coinage, Roman pottery in India is the artefact type to have attracted the most attention and to have been used most extensively to document Indo-Roman trade. Its identification is more problematic than that of coins since pottery is difficult to classify by description alone, and sometimes even from photographs or drawings, particularly in the case of body sherds.

Only through recent excavations on the Egyptian Red Sea coast has Indian pottery been recognised in the Roman world. Whitcomb (1982: 67) was the first to make tentative identifications from Myos Hormos, but a range of Indian vessels is now securely recognised on the basis of form and fabric (Tomber 2000). Furthermore, while studying the Egyptian assemblages it was possible for me to identify ceramics from Mesopotamia, East Africa and South Arabia. Here the main types and source areas of pottery that travelled throughout the Indian Ocean are described, although other unidentified types remain to be studied in more detail. The distribution patterns of these main wares, from both the Red Sea and beyond, will be discussed more fully in subsequent chapters as they make visible the interaction between political systems and ethnic groups.

Source identification of pottery can be determined in a number of ways, with the best results through the combination of vessel form and clay fabric. The study of clay fabrics is borrowed from geology and is based particularly on the identification of aplastic inclusions in the clay, either by eye or using a binocular or petrological microscope. The last enables the most precise classification of rocks and minerals and this technique was used extensively for identification of the fabrics described below. Sometimes sources can be assigned by matching the fabric with geological deposits, for which a geological map is invaluable. However, many mineral inclusions – such as quartz – are ubiquitous. In these cases typology is essential, for source areas can be suggested through distribution, with the greatest concentration likely to be in the home area. Nevertheless, pottery shapes are imitated outside their region for a variety of reasons, and detection of this relies on fabric analysis.

*Amphorae* (Figs 3-4)

A wide range of genuine Roman amphorae has been identified throughout the Indian Ocean. However, I have found that many amphorae in India, previously identified as Roman, actually comprise vessels of Mesopotamian origin.

A handle-less amphora, previously recorded in India as Roman, is not paralleled among Roman types. It has a distinctive tall, narrow base and barrel-shaped body, torpedo-like in shape. The fabric is unlike typical Indian ones, but not dissimilar to the Late Roman Amphora 1 (LR1) fabric, although it is generally fine and better sorted with finger impressions rather than wheelmarks on the inside. This so-called 'Torpedo jar' was produced between the late Parthian and Early Islamic periods and at least some of the vessels appear to have reached India during the Sasanian period (AD 224-651) (Tomber 2007b). Although no kilns are known, Mesopotamia is a likely source. A bitumen lining (Stern et al. 2008), visible on most vessels, indicates that they were used for the transportation of liquid. Like their Roman counterparts they probably contained wine, as a wine-drinking culture

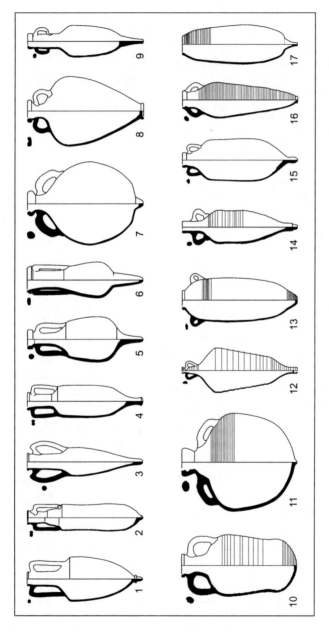

Fig. 3. Amphora types found throughout the Mediterranean and Indian Ocean (not to scale). For sources see Endnote 1. *Early Roman*: 1. Knidian; 2. Koan; 3. Rhodian; 4. Dressel 2-4; 5. Dressel 6A; 6. Dressel 7-11, 38; 7. Dressel 20; 8. Gauloise 4; 9. Amphore Egyptienne 3; *Late Roman*: 10. LR1; 11. LR2; 12. LR3; 13. LR4; 14. LR7; 15. Africano Grande; 16. *Aqaba*; *Mesopotamian*: 17. Torpedo.

*2. Charting exchange through texts and objects*

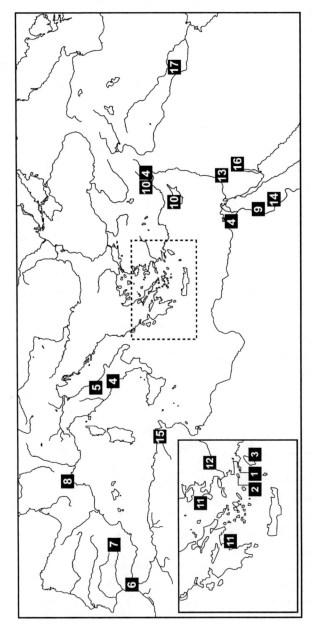

Fig. 4. Map showing the source areas for amphora types illustrated in Fig. 3.

41

existed in Mesopotamia (Simpson 2003: 353-5). The thick black lining helps to distinguish Torpedo sherds, for in India this is much better preserved than on Roman vessels. These may well be the containers for Persian wine mentioned in *PME* 36 and, of the pottery types outlined in this section, the Torpedo has not been positively identified on Red Sea sites, a point that we will return to later.

Another handle-less amphora is a conical-shaped vessel found particularly in South India during the Early Historic period, and not yet recognised outside India. At Kanchipuram in Tamil Nadu more than 50 were inset into the ground and perhaps used as storage jars for wine or toddy (a local sap-based drink) (Raman 1992: 127). The jars, known as Wheeler Type 74/5, based on Wheeler's Arikamedu typology (Wheeler et al. 1946: fig. 29), had an obvious use as storage vessels, but it is intriguing to speculate whether they mirrored their Roman counterparts as transport vessels. While in some of the older literature they are described as Roman, their Indian origin has been accepted for some time.

The range of Roman amphorae throughout the Indian Ocean incorporates vessels used for the transport of the three main commodities that formed the staples of Roman life: wine, oil and *garum*. Prior to the 1990s, and the reassessment of assemblages from Arikamedu (Will 1992; Slane 1992), no amphorae from India were precisely identified to source and could be understood only more generally from illustrations (particularly Wheeler et al. 1946: figs 9-10). We now know that amphorae from the Western and Eastern Mediterranean and the Red Sea were present in India, spanning between the first century BC and the sixth or seventh century AD.

Systematic classification of Roman amphorae began with Heinrich Dressel's typology of 1899, which still forms the basis for modern studies. As a result the dating, source and distribution of many types is well-known and need not be summarised. A varied terminology has grown up, and the ones used here rely on names in common usage (Keay & Williams 2005 for full terminology), with Late Roman (LR) and Dressel typologies consistently employed.

The main amphora shapes found throughout the Indian Ocean, and their production areas, are shown in Figs 3 and 4. Amphora shapes may or may not be exclusive to a single production area or fabric. One of the most popular Early Roman amphorae, Dressel's Types 2-4, was produced in most Roman provinces, but originated from an earlier Greek amphora made on Kos – the Koan amphora. Although it is a simple matter to identify the Dressel 2-4 when a handle or base is present, fabric is necessary to distinguish the specific source area. Even with visual inspection and petrographic analysis, it can be difficult to attribute some sherds to source area. Slane noted the problem of distinguishing the Koan fabric from some western Dressel 2-4s, while Whitbread's petrographic work indicated an overlap between Koan and other eastern fabrics (Slane 1992: 204; Whitbread 1995: 99). In the case of Koan amphorae, typology and stamps remain an important means for identification. Other fabrics can also be difficult to attribute to production area (particularly body sherds), but the establishment of an ongoing fabric database of samples from India provides a framework for classification as new sherds are recovered.

*Other Roman pottery*

In addition to amphorae, other classes of Roman pottery occur around the Indian Ocean. These include fine wares, such as *sigillata* from the Western and Eastern Mediterranean, as well as coarse table wares, particularly from Egypt. Unlike amphorae, which were traded for their contents, rationale for their export needs to be individually assessed. The main *sigillata* types encountered here are Italian (ITS), Eastern *Sigillata* A (ESA) from northern Syria, and Eastern *Sigillata* B (ESB) from Western Asia Minor, particularly the region of Ephesus.

## *India*

As well as the conical amphorae, in the past other Indian pottery types have been considered Roman (e.g. Singh 1977-8). The most persistent of these is the Rouletted Ware dish (RW; Fig. 5, no. 1) or Wheeler Type 1 (Wheeler et al. 1946: fig. 12), whose fine quality black and/or red/orange slipped fabric and decoration has contributed to this misattribution. In 1988 Begley presented strong arguments for an Indian production. Apparent fabric similarities between the classic rouletted fabric and the earlier, Indian Northern Black Polished Ware (NBP), and dissimilarities in form with Roman types, lent force to Begley's argument. In parallel, the same forms in coarse ware fabrics were recognised as Indian.

Begley considered RW a South Indian product, largely on distributional and typological grounds (2004b). A number of scientific analyses have confirmed that a single source region may be responsible for Rouletted and related wares (e.g. Ford et al. 2005). X-ray diffraction conducted by Gogte provided uniform results for RW samples from throughout India, Sri Lanka and Vietnam, NBP and clay from Chandra-ketugarh (1997, 2001). From this Gogte identified the Ganges Delta as the most likely source with the epicentre in the Chandraketugarh-Tamluk area. On personal examination, the large quantity of Rouletted and other fine grey wares from Chandraketugarh appear visually similar to those from Egypt, Arikamedu and other Indian sites.

While the Indian origin of RW is now accepted (Suresh 2004:

90), the inspiration for rouletted decoration, which was a common practice on both Greek and Roman pottery, remains unclear. Opinion varies on the dating of RW, the widest bracket being 400 BC-AD 300 (Ford et al. 2005: 911). Commonly it is placed between the second century BC and the first century AD (Suresh 2004: 98), although based on Arikamedu Begley considered it to be first century BC to third century AD (2004b: 639-40). Most recently Schenk has argued that production ceased in the first century BC (2006: 136-8). In all dating schemes, the first occurrence of RW predates Roman *sigillata* in India. Slane allied the style of rouletting, not placed between concentric circles, instead with Hellenistic black wares (1992: 212). Another suggestion, requiring further investigation, is that rouletting originated via the Gulf (Salles 2002: 199).

In her excellent reappraisal of the ware, Schenk has published an updated distribution map showing that RW followed both coastal and river paths. Curiously it has concentrations in Bangladesh and West Bengal, followed by an absence before resurfacing in peninsular India (2006: fig. 3). She suggests that Wheeler 1 and a few other forms (including Fig. 5, no. 2) in the same fabric were produced in the north specifically for the southern market (ibid.: 138-41). This would account for both its distribution and the distinct combination of

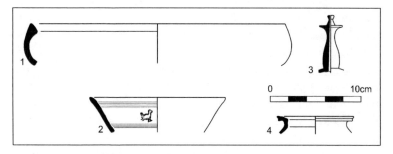

Fig. 5. Indian Fine Wares.
1-2. Rouletted and Related Ware from Myos Hormos; 3-4. Red Polished Ware from Gujarat (after Subbarao 1953: figure 24, no. 1; figure 26, no. 34).

red-and-black colours on the vessels, a technology associated with Megalithic coarse wares in southern India. Furthermore, she suggests that its distribution results primarily from gift exchange, related to the spread of Buddhism or Mauryan diplomatic activities, rather than through Indo-Roman trade (see also Gogte 1997: 81-2). However, a different explanation may apply to vessels imported into Egypt (Chapter 3, p. 74).

Another Indian fine ware historically considered Roman is Red Polished Ware (RPW; Fig. 5, nos 3-4) – here the confusion with Roman wares arose because of the similarity of its surface with Roman red-slipped wares. Nevertheless, RPW consists of a radically different set of forms, the most characteristic the sprinkler (Fig. 5, no. 3). Gujarat is now generally accepted as the source for RPW, where it was produced between approximately the first and fifth centuries AD , although a revision into the eighth century may be indicated (Kennet 2004: 65-6). Unlike amphorae, it is fairly easy to identify RW and RPW from publication alone, and from this adjust the quantity of Roman pottery identified in India.

Indian coarse wares exported to the West are more difficult to provenance and date, since some were produced from the Early Historic period to the present day in both North and South India. Coarse red wares, frequently with red slip that may be burnished (Coarse Red-slipped Wares – CRSW), particularly fall into this category (Fig. 6). The most common forms paralleled to Wheeler et al.'s 1946 typology, are in decreasing order, the carinated jar known today as the *handi* (Wheeler Type 24, figs 19-20), casserole (Wheeler Type 25, fig. 21), flanged casserole or lid (Wheeler Types 28-9, fig. 22) and plain rim dish (Wheeler Types 4-6, figs 14-15). Vessels from the Red Sea are frequently sooted on the outside, establishing their use as cooking vessels.

The Wheeler Type 24s from the Red Sea were formed using at least two different techniques. The first displays internal

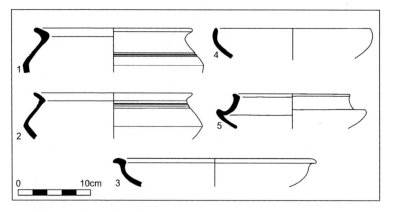

Fig. 6. Indian Coarse Red-slipped Wares from Berenike and Myos Hormos.
1-2. Wheeler Type 24; 3. Wheeler Type 25; 4. Wheeler Type 6; 5. Wheeler Type 29.

wiping with an organic material considered to be a by-product of bamboo tools, still used today in India (Tomber & Begley 2000: 156 and plate 3-4). Because of the distinctive nature of this wiping, it was hoped to source this pottery within India by locating parallels. With this aim, a search of collections from sites involved in Indo-Roman trade – such as Arikamedu, Nevasa and Nagara – was undertaken in 1998, but no matches were located. It was not until the site at Pattanam was discovered (see Chapter 5) and the pottery from it examined in late 2003 that a match was found. A return to the ethnographic literature was equally positive, describing a technique today known, only to the potters of North Kerala, as scooping. A ball of clay is roughly shaped, bamboo tools are then used to hollow the inside and define the rim and neck, followed by internal beating to achieve the correct thickness. Finally the vessel is burnished inside and out (Saraswati & Behura 1966: 81-3). It seems that the vessels found in Egypt and some seen in Kerala were less carefully finished, so that the bamboo marks are still visible. In this way a direct link between Kerala and the Red Sea was established. Different working techniques are visible on other CRSW sherds, but are less distinct than the organic marks and it has not yet been possible to locate their source within India. Nevertheless, petrographic examination of the Wheeler Type 24 and related forms found in Egypt confirms that numerous production centres were involved.

A coarse black, handmade fabric with very thick walls is also distinctive, and it too had a long production period in India (Organic Black Ware). Two main forms are found in small numbers throughout the Indian Ocean, a dish and a large jar, frequently sooted (Fig. 7, nos 1-3). Despite their thickness, the vessels are light in weight, so that when it was first encountered I nicknamed it 'light ware'. The fabric had been tracked previously in India by Sunil Gupta, whose own pet name for it was 'spongy ware'. The lightness results from its vesicular fabric caused by organic temper, particularly of rice (Fig. 8; Tomber et al. in preparation). In India the ware is found in the north-west, clustered in Gujarat at sites such as Kamrej. An unusual vessel form, Wheeler's Type 38 (Fig. 7, no. 5) was sometimes produced in this fabric, but variability demonstrates more than one production centre for it, including a potential one in the Nile Valley (Davidde & Petriaggi 1998: fig. 6, citing Bietak & Schwartz 1987: 191).

Additional Indian Coarse Wares have been identified outside the subcontinent, for which geographical sources can only be loosely suggested (Indian Coarse Wares, Fig. 7, no. 4, Figs 13-14). Most common are a range of unsooted jars interpreted as storage containers, which have wide-ranging parallels in India, both geographically and chronologically. A distinct subclass was produced using the paddle and anvil technique with a grooved paddle (Paddle Impressed Wares; Fig. 7, no. 6; Begley 2004c: 202-5; Selvakumar 2004: 616-17). Although the distribution for these jars is expanding, it is concentrated at east coast sites in India and in Sri Lanka, between the Early Historic and medieval/modern period. The

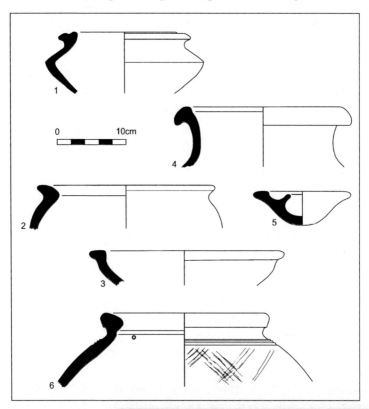

Fig. 7. Indian Coarse Wares from Berenike and Myos Hormos. 1-3. Organic Black Ware; 4. Indian Coarse Ware; 5. Wheeler Type 38; 6. Paddle Impressed Ware.

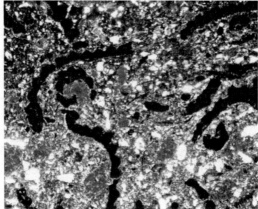

Fig. 8. Thin-section photomicrograph showing rice temper in Organic Black Ware from Berenike (field view 0.87 mm).

east coast is therefore considered its most likely source area, with fabrics identified in Egypt indicating sources from both South India and the Chandraketugarh region.

Although many of the Indian wares are difficult to source precisely, pottery from the north (RPW, Organic Black Ware), east (RW, Paddle Impressed Wares) and south-west (CRSW with organic impressions) are identified and provide some geographical control for assessing the embarkation point for Indian pottery.

### South Arabia

One pottery type from South Arabia has quantitatively significant distribution outside the region. This is a group of high-footed storage jars in calcareous clay, frequently iron free, with organic tempering (Organic Storage Jars; Fig. 9, nos 1-2). While the fabric is not dissimilar to some Egyptian ones, the form is distinct and parallels from the Hadramawt were drawn to my attention by Alexander Sedov. Further confirmation for a Yemeni source, where the type was produced between the late first century BC and the fourth or possibly early fifth century AD , comes from a vessel found in Egypt with a prefiring painted South Arabian graffito (Tomber 2004b: 353, fig. 6). Vessels are normally lined with a dark coating; using gas chromatography-mass spectrometry this coating has been identified by Rebecca Stacey as bitumen on some samples, beeswax on others. Their function as containers for liquid is reinforced by remnants of plaster seal around the mouth and they may have been used for either water (Sedov & Benvenuti 2002: 194) or Arabian wine mentioned in *PME* 49.

A whole-mouth cooking pot with lug handles similar in shape to stone bowls from South Arabia is tentatively identified as having a Yemeni source, through comparison with prehistoric fabrics provided by Alexandra Porter from Little

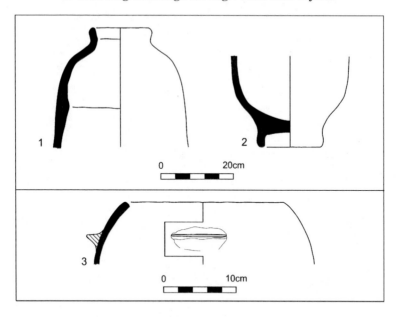

Fig. 9. South Arabian Wares from Myos Hormos.
1-2. Organic Storage Jars; 3. Whole-mouth Cooking pot.

Aden (Whole-mouth Cooking pot; Fig. 9, no. 3; Tomber 2004b: 355-7). The fabric is basaltic and consultation with geological maps shows Aden, an important region for Indo-Roman trade, to have suitable natural resources.

## Mesopotamia and the Gulf

Mesopotamian Torpedo jars have already been described above. Another pottery type from this region is a turquoise, alkaline Glazed Ware thought to be produced around Basra (Fig. 10). With production continuing over a long period of time, possibly from as early as the third century BC into the Early Islamic period (Kennet 2004: 29-30), vessels are difficult to date unless specific shapes or decoration are present. Other

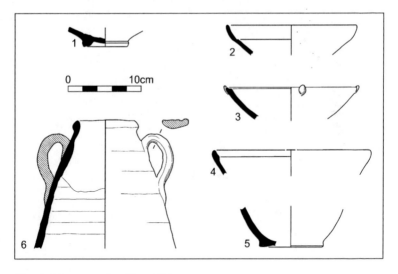

Fig. 10. Mesopotamian Glazed Ware.
1-2. Myos Hormos; 3-6. Berenike.

ware types, represented by rare sherds, may have reached the Red Sea via the Gulf from neighbouring regions, but are not described here.

### East Africa

Classic Aksumite pottery has a distinctive repertoire that made it fairly easy to recognise decorated sherds at the Red Sea sites (Aksumite Coarse Wares; Fig. 11, 3-6). Nevertheless, it was important to confirm that the vessels were actually from East Africa rather than an East African style made in Egypt. Invaluably, sherds and thin sections from Aksum itself were made available to me for comparison by David Phillipson and Jacke Phillips. Thus far two main fabrics have been identified from the Roman world and both are likely to be Aksumite in origin. The first has mudstone and trachytic igneous inclusions and compares well with samples from Aksum; the second fabric

52

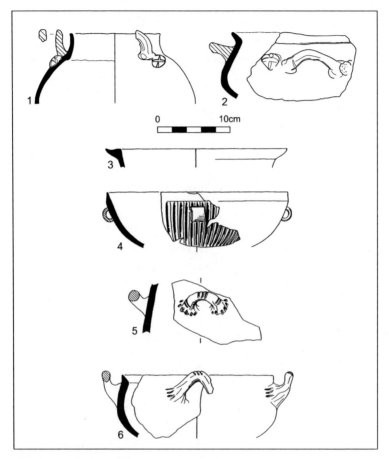

Fig. 11. East African Wares.
1-2. Sandy Red Ware from Myos Hormos; 3-6. Aksumite Coarse Wares from Berenike.

is micaceous with lightly metamorphosed rocks, and while not represented among the Aksum samples, is geologically compatible within the region (Tomber 2005b: 46).

A third fabric has distinctive calcareous, granitic-tempered clay and is decorated with incised bosses known in the Aksumite repertoire (Red Sandy Ware; Fig. 11, nos 1-2; ibid.:

53

43-5). This combination of form and fabric is not known at Aksum. Geological maps show a suitable area in the region surrounding Asmara and Massawa, north of the *Periplus* port of Adulis, where there is a juncture of sedimentary and volcanic resources. The Red Sandy vessels are frequently sooted from their use as cooking pots. The function of the classic Aksumite pots is less certain, but some were used over fire.

## Natural products

As distinct from pottery, natural products such as spices and aromatics were the driving force of Indian Ocean commerce. Less durable than other materials, the dry conditions in the Eastern Desert of Egypt has greatly facilitated archaeo-botanical research (Chapter 3, Table 1). This is demonstrated particularly through the work of René Cappers and Marijke Van der Veen, who have identified numerous plant remains, some of which are itemised in documents (Wendrich et al. 2003: table 2).

Most products can be tied to main growing regions, but are difficult to source more precisely. Frankincense, for instance, is native to both Yemen and Somalia. The documents confused questions of source, with the provenance of goods equated with the port where they were acquired. Inexact geography, distorting the relationship between different regions, as discussed above, may have exacerbated the problem. Cinnamon is a complex example, and has received much attention (Miller 1969: 42-7; 74-7; 153-72; De Romanis 1996; Goyon 2005; Amigues 2005). It seems that true cinnamon came from the Malabar Coast and Sri Lanka, along with its poorer grade *cassia*, which was also available from Southeast Asia and southern China (Dalby 2000: 38; Cappers 2006: 10-11). Strabo (*Geography* 2.5.7, 2.5.35) considered its source East Africa, while Pliny (*NH* 12.85-8) apparently understood that it was acquired in East Africa via South Arabian middlemen from very far away in the East (Miller 1969: 155-7).

There are, of course, exceptions where growing areas are more restricted and sourcing more exact. Pepper is the best example of this, with products from North and South India distinguishable. Two species of pepper were available from India: from the north-east was *Piper longum* (long pepper), and from the south-west, *Piper nigrum* (black pepper). A third type mentioned in the documents was white pepper, ripe black pepper without the outer skin. Long pepper is the hotter of the two and was favoured particularly for medicinal purposes (Dalby 2000: 90). Both the writer of the *Periplus* (*PME* 56) and Pliny (*NH* 6.105) knew that some pepper came from Kerala, respectively described as Kottanarike/Cottonara. *PME* 49 also described the export of long pepper from Barygaza. According to Pliny (*NH* 12.26-9) black pepper was the cheapest at 4D per Roman pound, with white at 7D and long at 15D, but he assumed that they all belonged to the same plant (Cappers 2006: 112). The exemption of black pepper in the Alexandrian tariff might, by modern standards, imply it was a staple. At present only black, no long or white, pepper has been found in an archaeological context, although preservation makes white difficult to verify (Cappers 2006: 114-19).

Because of the exceptional preservation conditions, over 95% of the pepper recovered from archaeological contexts in the Roman world comes from the Eastern Desert of Egypt; in Europe only odd grains of black pepper have been recovered (ibid.). Indirect evidence is instead important for establishing its use. One example is the *horrea piperataria* north of the Sacra Via in Rome established by Dominitian and used for the storage and possibly sale of Oriental spices and pepper (Rickman 1971: 105-6, 170); fourth-century silver pepper pots from Hoxne, Suffolk are another (Johns forthcoming).

## From provenance to trade routes

The ability to provenance archaeological remains is a critical first step in any attempt to reconstruct ancient trade, by enabling artefacts outside their home market to be identified. Nevertheless, simple matching of find spots and sources does not necessarily trace the routes by which they travelled. Assessing the quantity of objects can go some way towards addressing this problem. However, the presence of Roman objects, for example, need not equate with the presence of Romans (e.g. Salles 1993: n. 46). Not only were indirect routes frequently advantageous, but entrepots for the collection and redistribution of goods an important feature of the ancient economy. Within the Roman sphere, Alexandria can be readily identified as a regional entrepot through both historical sources and the richness of its artefact assemblages (e.g. Bonifay & Leffy 2002; Majcherek 2004). Sites containing a wide variety of goods are strong contenders for entrepots or emporia and this criterion can be used to define them in South Arabia and India.

Another aspect that will be developed in subsequent chapters is the meaning of imported goods. While relevant within the Roman Empire, it becomes more so for external cultures. What, for example, was the meaning of Roman wine in India? Was it intended for locals or foreigners, were the contents enjoyed by a range of consumers? If not enjoyed, were they valued in another way, perhaps bestowing status on the owner? (Moreland 2003: 28ff., 80). In this chapter the complementary input of documents, coins, pottery and archaeobotany has been emphasised. As we shall see, other categories of finds also elucidate the interconnections between regions.

# 3

# Evolution of the Roman Red Sea

In the complex network of regions it is the Red Sea that served as a funnel for goods from the East to the Roman Empire. Two arteries were available: in the west through six ports that connected with the Nile via a series of desert stations and eventually onwards to Alexandria, and in the east where two ports channelled goods to Gaza. An obvious question is why so many trade ports were needed for the Red Sea and how they related to each other functionally and chronologically.

## The ports (Fig. 12)

### From the land of the Pharaohs

The western Roman Red Sea is contained within modern Egypt. Ptolemy (*Geography* 4.5.8) lists six harbours, from north to south as Clysma, Myos Hormos, Philoteras, Leukos Limen, Nechesia and Berenike. By the late 1980s Clysma, Leukos Limen and Berenike had been located (Sidebotham 1992), but since then intense exploration has radically changed our understanding of this landscape. Today we can identify Clysma, Berenike and possibly Nechesia, while the modern site of Quseir al-Qadim, which was thought to be Leukos Limen, is now confirmed as Myos Hormos.

In the mid-first century the *Periplus* mentions only Myos Hormos and Berenike (*PME* 1, 19). Earlier, Strabo (*Geography* 17.1.45) described Myos Hormos as the more important of the two and it was from here that Aelius Gallus returned after his

57

aborted South Arabian mission in 24 BC (*Geography* 16.4.24).
Only recently has Myos Hormos been securely identified:
from the first half of the nineteenth century Abu Shaar was
considered the most likely candidate for this port (Wellstead
1838, cited by Sidebotham 1992: 17). Five seasons of
excavation at Abu Shaar from 1987 validated its role in
long-distance commerce – through a gate inscription reading
'*ad usum mercatorum*' (Bagnall & Sheridan 1994: 162-3;
Sidebotham 1994: 141, 158) – but not as a port. Sidebotham
uncovered a fort that was established in the early fourth
century and modified into a Christian church in the late fourth
or early fifth, before the site was eventually abandoned
sometime during or after the sixth century. Although located to
monitor international trade and police nomads in the vicinity,
its chronology rules out activity during the time of the *Periplus*
and thus its viability as Myos Hormos.

Comparison of ancient descriptions of Myos Hormos with
modern satellite images led David Peacock to the now accepted
conclusion that modern Quseir al-Qadim was the ancient site
of Myos Hormos, not Leukos Limen (1993). Subsequent
excavation between 1999 and 2003 by David Peacock and Lucy
Blue of the University of Southampton confirmed this
hypothesis through a variety of written evidence, including a
papyrus that mentions 'Myos Hormos at the Red Sea' (Van
Rengen 2000: 51); elsewhere in the Eastern Desert, at al-Zerqa
on the Coptos-Myos Hormos road, an *ostracon* indicates that
Myos Hormos was the terminus of that road (Bülow-Jacobsen
et al. 1994). Where then should we find Leukos Limen? The
consensus, at the moment, is that Ptolemy inadvertently
confused Leukos Limen with Leuke Kome in Saudi Arabia
(ibid.: n. 7; Cuvigny 2003: 28-30), setting modern scholars off
on a search for a non-existent site on the western Red Sea.

Earlier excavations by the University of Chicago had
identified two major structural periods at Myos Hormos, an

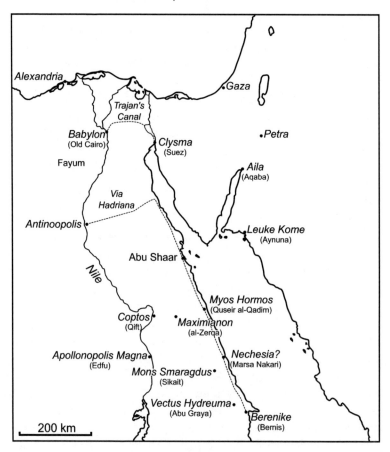

Fig. 12. Map of the Roman Red Sea region.

Early Roman one from the first century AD to late second or early third century, followed by a period of abandonment prior to Mamluk occupation (Whitcomb & Johnson 1979, 1982). For the Roman sequence they uncovered a number of buildings, including what was interpreted as a *horreum* with attached shops and a fort (Whitcomb 1996), but the identification of the fort cannot be sustained (Peacock & Blue 2006: 5-6).

59

The University of Southampton excavations were able to refine this chronology, identifying deposits between the late Augustan period and what appears to be the mid-third century AD. Whitcomb and Johnson's results hinted at some Ptolemaic occupation through one coin of Ptolemy III (Sidebotham 1992: n. 44). Ptolemaic finds recovered residually by Southampton included three coins of the second and first centuries BC (D. Peacock, pers. comm.) and rare sherds of Ptolemaic pottery that reinforce the possibility of an earlier foundation for the site. How early is not clear, although both Strabo (*Geography* 16.4.5) and Pliny (*NH* 6.168) put it around the same time as Berenike.

A major aim of the Southampton excavations was to locate the now silted-up ancient harbour. Blue conducted sedimentological analysis on over 100 2 x 2 m test pits on the south and eastern limits of the site to trace a southern channel connecting the sea to the harbour situated east of the town (Blue 2006: figs 4.4, 4.14). From these test pits and adjacent excavations a remarkable feature was uncovered – an area over 60 m in length consisting of hundreds of complete to near-complete pots, many in upright positions. Interpretation altered as they slowly revealed themselves, until eventually it was clear that they were laid to form a jetty (see front cover) and also to consolidate waterlogged land, as a 'hard' (an artificial foreshore or landing place) (Peacock & Blue 2006: 67-74). Most of the pots were Roman amphorae of Egyptian and Italian origin dating to the late Augustan period, but occasional jugs and other vessels – including a complete South Arabian Organic Storage Jar – occurred alongside. The fill surrounding the vessels contained sherds, including some potential Ptolemaic ones, and it is in this area, in submerged deposits, that Ptolemaic levels may lie. More purpose-built structures were not entirely absent, and a stone harbour wall was constructed elsewhere, probably during the second century (ibid.: 176).

## 3. Evolution of the Roman Red Sea

What is perhaps most striking about the site is the lack of a well-established street system and substantial architecture (ibid.), despite its prominent role as attested in the documents and in its occupation for over 200 years. A single monumental structure with dressed limestone foundations and mudbrick walls was excavated by Southampton. Remnants of stucco (with some Greek graffiti), plaster moulding and half a pillar made of stone and coral that would have been finished with plaster were also recovered. One tentative interpretation is that the building was a synagogue; certainly there was a Hebrew *ostracon* on site (Copeland 2006: 125-7 and citing W. Van Rengen, pers. comm.). Most of the other buildings were of mudbrick, sometimes in combination with coral and ashlar. Areas for baking and activities related to fishing were identified; another for smithing seems, by its pottery, to be associated with East African and Indian foreigners (Thomas & Masser 2006: 133, 137-8; Thomas 2007: 154-6).

The ephemeral nature of Myos Hormos may reflect its position on the edge of the Empire. This contrasts with Berenike, another port of the *Periplus*, located 300 km further south. A sequence from the mid-third century BC into the early sixth century AD has been identified from eight excavation seasons conducted by the Universities of Delaware and Leiden and published by Sidebotham and Wendrich (1995, 1996, 1998, 1999, 2000, 2007). Here, at least for the Late Roman period, was a Hippodamian street grid system; stone architecture was fairly common, composed, as at Myos Hormos, of ashlar or coral from the adjacent reef (called *opus Berenikeum*), or mudbrick (Sidebotham 2002: 233). Staircases revealed the presence of two-storey buildings, probably serving commercial or public functions on ground level and domestic or private above. Small metal scales and weights found in narrow entrances at street level indicate offices or shops dealing with valuable, light-weight items (ibid.: 220-1).

The lay-out of Berenike shows a shift in the settlement from Ptolemaic to Late Roman times, gradually migrating eastwards and southwards with the most intensive occupation from the mid-fourth century onwards (ibid.). This movement was in part a response to silting from the wadi and the shore. The harbour, although never dredged, was not as thoroughly silted as that at Myos Hormos and essentially still follows the same line as in Antiquity. A wide range of activities are evident, such as light industry (e.g. iron working), a cemetery, and numerous architectural features including a quay wall, a warehouse, and temples or shrines celebrating different cults, including Serapis, Palmyrene and Nubian. The largest religious building, thought to accommodate between 75 and 80 worshippers, was a fifth/sixth-century purpose-built church with an aisled hall containing eight pillars. A room on the west had benches and a number of dolia and amphorae suggest food consumption, which would have been prepared in a northern annexe. Within the aisled hall were bronze and ceramic lamps with Christian motifs; one lamp from Aswan carries the Christian motto 'Jesus save me' (Sidebotham & Wendrich 2001-2: 32-4, fig. 21).

While Late Roman Berenike presents itself as a substantial community with a degree of town planning, so far no streets have been excavated for earlier periods and it is unclear whether they existed or, if so, on the same plan (Sidebotham 2002: 229). Equally, there were few structures, apart from harbour installations and the temple of Serapis (ibid.: 220). Strabo (*Geography* 7.17.45) described Berenike as a landing place, rather than a harbour. It may be that during the Early Roman period there was less investment in the ports, but that the Late Roman period saw a shift in organisation or available funds that encouraged development. On the face of it, this is in opposition to the cultural cycle proposed for Berenike based on faunal remains and pottery, which indicate a gradual decline in the Romanised population and an increase in Egyptian and desert dwellers during Late Roman times (Sidebotham 2004: 112-13).

A key question that concerns scholars is why two ports – Myos Hormos and Berenike – were needed in such proximity to one another. The northerly winds of the Red Sea are infamous and they have been invoked frequently as one explanation for the more southerly location of Berenike (Casson 1989: 13). Additional upwind sailing from Berenike to Myos Hormos might, however, be compensated for by its greater proximity to the Nile port of Coptos. Of the two sea ports, Myos Hormos is the shortest distance from the Nile – between six and seven days' journey (Strabo *Geography* 17.1.45) in contrast to the 11 or 12 days needed from Berenike (Pliny *NH* 6.104). Whitewright has calculated a sailing time of between 24 hours and 5.5 days between the two ports, depending on the wind direction and conditions. He has further calculated three alternative land/sea routes for Berenike and Myos Hormos and concluded that in actual time there is little difference between them (2007a: 85-7). But, factoring in the ease of transport on sea as compared to land, in environmental and economic terms, Myos Hormos was by far the more efficient of the two ports. Why then Berenike? Whitewright argues that Indian skippered ships may have had more difficultly reaching Myos Hormos given their unfamiliarity with northerly winds and would have preferred stopping at Berenike. Social factors – such as family connections – may also have been a determinant (ibid.).

Berenike was at the terminus of the Via Hadriana, the coastal road that originated at Antinoopolis, turned eastwards and then loosely followed the coast south (Sidebotham et al. in preparation). Its main purpose is thought to have been military and administrative rather than commercial, although it would have expedited trade. Forts and watering stations provided the infrastructure between the ports and the Nile and they, as well as quarries such as the emerald mine at Sikait (Foster et al. 2007), attest to flourishing activity in the region. These desert sites, and their interlinking routes, are a subject in their own right that cannot be fully explored here (e.g. Cuvigny 2003).

The archaeological sequences for Myos Hormos and Berenike indicate some interplay in their roles and suggest that they were symbiotic. On archaeological evidence alone Berenike was the earlier foundation. It would have been an important port for the Ptolemaic elephant trade with Africa, which was government-instigated and primarily, but not exclusively, of a military character (Burstein 1996: 800). Although it probably had an earlier foundation, archaeological evidence is unequivocal that by the late first century BC/early first century AD Myos Hormos was firmly established. From this date into the Flavian period, both sites maintained robust populations. This is in keeping with both the *Periplus* and the Nicanor archive which implied that they were equally important (Casson 1989: 13). By the late first and second centuries AD the archaeological evidence is stronger from Myos Hormos than Berenike. In terms of overall evolution, this is at variance with Pliny (*NH* 6.101-6), whose silence regarding Myos Hormos suggests that, by the late 70s, it was declining in favour of Berenike (Warmington 1928: 7).

Various explanations have been sought for the dip in occupation at Berenike during the second century, including a widespread plague in Egypt from AD 166 (Sidebotham & Wendrich 1998: 453-4), but this dip was not mirrored at Myos Hormos. Instead, based on the ceramics, it appears that during the second century and the first half of the third century Myos Hormos was much more intensively used than Berenike and that the silting up of the Myos Hormos harbour sometime during the third century reversed this trend. Third- and early fourth-century material is ill-defined at Berenike, but by the mid- to late fourth century the site was again thriving and Myos Hormos was abandoned. In this context it is interesting to note that contrary to documentary evidence, during the second and early third centuries the Myos Hormos-Nile road network was denser than the Berenike one (Cuvigny 2005: 36-7). A hiatus during the second half of the third century may have resulted from the general disruption throughout the Empire during this period (Sidebotham & Wendrich ibid.), and the brief disruption caused by Diocletian's temporary destruction of Coptos in AD 292 (Young 2001: 86).

Also to be considered are the Egyptian ports not mentioned in the *Periplus* but in Ptolemy's *Geography* (4.5.8): Nechesia and Clysina (Clysma). Nechesia may equate to the modern site at Marsa Nakari, located approximately equidistant between Myos Hormos and Berenike, where one excavation season has been conducted (Seeger 2001: 77). Although the finds have not yet been systematically studied, a sequence from at least the late first (*c.* AD 69/70) to the late fourth century (*c.* AD 361) is indicated by coins (ibid.: 84-5); the presence of LR1 (S. Sidebotham, pers. comm.) suggests that it was also occupied during the fifth century. Superficially, in terms of architecture visible on the surface and in the excavated trenches, Marsa Nakari has more in common with Berenike than with Myos Hormos. If the co-existence of Myos Hormos and Berenike is perplexing, the addition of a third site into the equation during the Early Roman period is even more so. If its zenith belonged to the Late Roman period, when Myos Hormos had ceased to function, the possibility exists that for each main period a back-up or auxiliary port was maintained for unfavourable weather conditions. Marsa Nakari certainly had a good harbour; our understanding of its relationship to other ports awaits further excavation.

Three ancient sites are known in the vicinity of modern Suez and of these only Clysma can be precisely located at Tell

Qulzum (Bruyère 1966). Here a westerly canal connected the Red Sea and the Nile, terminating at Babylon (Old Cairo). The complex history of the canal – at least from Darius I (522-486 BC) and possibly from Pharaonic times – has recently been summarised by Cooper (2005). It seems to have been active during the Ptolemaic period from the third century BC, but no longer navigable by the first century BC, when Strabo (*Geography* 16.4.23, 17.1.25) described the building of the fleet for South Arabia by Aelius Gallus on the 'old canal' at a nearby site, referred to as Cleopatris. The Roman re-excavation is attributed to Trajan, resulting in the epithet 'River of Trajan'. Its exploitation continued until at least the early fifth and possibly into the late sixth century, if Gregory of Tours' *Historia Francorum* was based on contemporary accounts (Cooper 2005: 44-5). If indeed it was dredged under Trajan, there are at least 100 years when the canal was not functional for Eastern trade. When functional it allowed the entire journey from Alexandria to the Red Sea and beyond to be made by water, apart from loading at various junctures, as noted in the late second century:

> What happened was this. The young man cruised up the Nile as far as Clysma, and as a vessel was just putting to sea, was induced to join others in a voyage to India (Lucian *Alexander the False Prophet* 44).

The fourth century and later were periods of intense activity at Clysma and Aila (below). French excavations of the 1930s at Tell Qulzum revealed a sequence spanning the Ptolemaic through Islamic periods; of the pre-Islamic sequence, the Ptolemaic and Late Roman were best represented and there are thousands of coins dated to the fourth and fifth centuries (Bruyère 1966: 90-5; Young 2001: 77, 86). Up to the fifth or early sixth century, occupation therefore overlapped with

Berenike. In 1925 Bourdon observed a number of architectural features at the site, including port infrastructure and what he took to be a Justinianic church (Cooper 2005: 81). Today much of the site is hidden by urban sprawl although a lagoon feature is visible (ibid.: 59).

The twelfth-century text of Peter the Deacon credits Egeria the nun with this description of Clysma in the late fourth century:

> ... it receives ships from India, for ships from India can come to no other port but this in Roman territory. And the ships there are numerous and great, since it is a port renowned for the Indian merchants who come to it. Also the official [*agens in rebus*] known as the *logotherte* [auditor or assessor] has his residence there, the one who goes on embassy each year to India by order of the Roman emperor ... (*Itinerarium Egeriae* 6.4.7, trans. Wilkinson 1981: 206).

Mayerson has questioned whether this is Egeria's description from the late fourth century or derived from Placentius' sixth-century observations, and furthermore whether it refers to East Africa rather than India (1996). The martyr Antoninus Placentius' account of *c.* AD 570 described the arrival of Indian ships at Aila and Clysma, but his one mention of pepper, which just might indicate true India, was not in reference to these ports (*Itinerarium* 40-1, trans. J.P. Wild). The finds from Clysma do little to establish its role in Indo-Roman trade, but indicate that the town was flourishing when Egeria visited. The greater distance between Berenike and Clysma than between Berenike and Myos Hormos makes the location of Clysma more understandable, despite the need to travel further against the northerly winds to reach it.

## *Nabataean to Roman*

The eastern side of the Red Sea was integral to both the seaborne trade and overland routes for the aromatics trade that was particularly served by the port of Leuke Kome (Young 2001: 96). In reference to the campaign of Aelius Gallus, Strabo (*Geography* 16.4.23) described Leuke Kome as a large emporium. *PME* 19 describes it as a port for small craft from Arabia on their way to Petra, a route that may have gone via Aila (Casson 1989: 144), although Aila is not mentioned in the *Periplus*. Furthermore, *PME* 19 mentions that a customs officer and a centurion were present at Leuke Kome; one interpretation of this is that the site was under Roman control at the time. Sidebotham has argued that both these titles may have been used by Nabataeans as well as Romans, while Young sees Leuke Kome as a Nabataean port with a Roman presence to ensure that goods entering the port did not escape the quarter tax levied on goods coming into the Empire (Sidebotham 1986: 106-7; Young 1997).

Archaeologically Leuke Kome has been identified as a cluster of seven inter-related settlements in the region of Aynuna in Saudi Arabia, *c.* 5 km from the coast at the mouth of the Gulf of Aqaba (Ingraham et al. 1981: 76-8). Although known only through survey, extensive architecture is visible at two of the complexes, including a standing tower; nearby is a large necropolis. It seems that during the first century AD there was some decline in the use of Leuke Kome as a result of the ascendancy of the Egyptian maritime routes, but that it continued to play a role in the still robust overland trade (Young 2001: 100, 103-4). Leuke Kome is described in the mid-third-century *Monumentum Adulitanum* (Chapter 4, 88-9), which implies that it was still active at that time as part of *Provincia Arabia*. A reference by Marcianus may extend the occupation until AD 400 (Ward 2002: 115).

## 3. Evolution of the Roman Red Sea

Surface pottery from Aynuna included Nabataean wares (Ingraham et al. 1981: pls 82, 86), but no Egyptian or Eastern ones can be identified from the literature. Petra, the capital of Nabataea and an important caravan site, has, on the other hand, been intensively excavated and published. To date, Gogte (1999) has identified a mould-decorated pot similar to Hellenistic ones, like those made in western India (Begley 1992: 157-76). There is a potential for the recovery of further Indian and Arabian finds from these sites, which will help to clarify their role on the wider maritime stage.

The site at Aila in Jordan is much better known than Clysma. Its importance as a long-distance port can be traced to the late third century, but before that it played a vital role in overland caravan routes and the frankincense trade via Leuke Kome and more directly from Saudi Arabia (Ward 2007: 163). Its early non-port status is reinforced by its absence from the *Periplus*. Strabo (*Geography* 16.2.30) described Aila as a city at the head of the Arabian Gulf, connected to Gaza by a desert road that was used for the transportation of aromatics (*Geography* 16.4.4). In the early fourth century Eusebius of Caesarea recorded its role as a port for India via Egypt in his *Onomasticon* (Freeman-Grenville et al. 2003: 14) and Placentius mentioned it in tandem with trade at Clysma. Eastern goods may have reached Aila indirectly via Adulis (Chapter 4, p. 93).

This link between Aila and Clysma relates not only to their geographical proximity, but also to their shared history, as both continued into the seventh century after the abandonment of Berenike. Ward has argued that Clysma and Aila may have remained active longer than Berenike because of internal security threats from nomads that made ports in the northern Red Sea easier to secure than the more isolated Berenike (2007).

Six seasons of excavation by Tom Parker of North Carolina

69

State University have provided an archaeological sequence from the first-century BC Nabataean settlement through to the seventh century, continuing as the Islamic town of Ayla (1996, 1998, 2000, 2002, 2003). A break around the turn of the second century may be related to the Roman annexation; alternatively it may have been caused by an earthquake (Thomas et al. 2007: 63). Parker's excavations uncovered a single monumental building and domestic mudbrick ones; there is also some evidence for commercial bakeries, and pottery production was indicated by waste heaps rather than actual kilns. The port itself was available for investigation only from 2003 and findings have not yet been published (R. Thomas, pers. comm.).

Mudbrick domestic architecture continued into the Late Roman/Byzantine period, as did stone structures, including domestic buildings and a town wall. Importantly a new monumental building was constructed over the Nabataean one, this later one interpreted as a church. The largest structure on site, it had ashlar foundations with mudbrick upper walls and an eastern orientation. Its construction is dated to the turn of the fourth century, which, if it is a church, would make it the earliest in Jordan (Parker 2003: 326). This identification has been controversial, but in addition to its orientation, associated artefacts lend support. These include glass lamps and fragments from a cage cup, and possibly an offering table (ibid.: 325-6). A wooden box containing 100 coins dating to around 360 has been tentatively interpreted as a collection box (Parker 2000: 383). Although the building suffered extensively from an earthquake in the mid-fourth century, it remained in use until the late fourth century when a second quake caused it to be essentially abandoned, although part of it was reused as a domestic structure (Thomas et al. 2007: 63-6). The adjacent fourth-century cemetery, oriented with the building, included a burial with a cross (Parker 2000: 383). Another important feature of Late Roman Aila was production of the widespread Aqaba amphora between the fourth and seventh centuries, possibly continuing into the Early Islamic period (Hayes 1996: table 6-10; Melkawi et al. 1994).

## Material remains (Table 1; see pp. 83-7)

Archaeological evidence for imported goods at the Egyptian sites during the Ptolemaic period is virtually non-existent. Ceramic deposits from Berenike dating to its foundation in the mid-third to the second century BC consist primarily of Egyptian vessels, with some imports from Rhodes. Rare elephant tusks, of either African or Indian species, were collected throughout the sequence, and a single tooth from a Ptolemaic deposit (Van Neer & Ervynck 1999: 331-2; 348; Sidebotham & Wendrich 2001-2: 41, citing Van Neer, pers. comm.), provide the only evidence for the import of elephants into Berenike as described by Agatharchides (Burstein 1989: 141-3).

It is not until the Augustan period that substantial assemblages are again represented and these are radically different, containing rich evidence for Eastern trade. During their period of co-occupation, particularly between the late first century BC and the late first century AD, Berenike and Myos Hormos shared an impressive range of Eastern imports from India, South Arabia and East Africa that are summarised together on Table 1. The more extensive list from Berenike would seem to result not from real differences but from the greater amount of excavation and publication to date.

From India alone, the list is long. Many of these items such as gems, spices and textiles were objects of trade and are well documented by the *Periplus* in relation to Egypt. Other goods are mentioned in the *Periplus*, but not as imports to Egypt: for example, *PME* 36 states that wood was exported from India to the Gulf. A third category of objects, including coconut, mung beans, glass beads and many pottery types, is known only

71

through excavation (Wendrich et al. 2003). This silence may represent items that were not systematically exchanged or used only by the crew during the voyage.

Gems belong to a category of non-essential luxury goods and a wide variety is present, sometimes as cameo blanks. These are not straightforward to source: carnelian, for example, occurs in both India and Egypt. Its source is most accurately identified by working techniques that can distinguish Egyptian from Indian and even between those from North and South India (Francis 2007: 254). A single bead from Java at Berenike illustrates indirect connections with Southeast Asia, although it may date to the early seventh century after the site was abandoned (ibid.: 254-5). More common are small, drawn glass 'Indo-Pacific' beads, which were produced in South India and Sri Lanka (Francis 2004: 450-1). First imported in small numbers during the Early Roman period, by the Late Roman period they accounted for approximately half of the beads at Berenike. Their colour suggests they were made at Mantai, Sri Lanka, rather than the other main production site of Arikamedu in India (Francis 2000: 222).

Foodstuffs are particularly interesting, in terms of their intended consumers – were they for trade or for the traders? Although rice was cultivated in the Near East at this time, it probably reached the Red Sea via the 'Far Side' ports such as Opone, exported from growing areas in Southeast Asia or India (*PME* 14, 31, 41; Cappers 2006: 104-5). It occurred in 'reasonable' quantities at Berenike and in small amounts at Myos Hormos (ibid.; Van der Veen 2004: 127). It may have been eaten mainly by resident Indians (a similar argument is presented for wheat on p. 148), but the evidence is more complicated since according to Apicius it was also used in Roman recipes as a thickening agent (Cappers ibid.).

*PME* 48 and 49 clearly distinguish between garments and cloth, also indicating the quality of those exported from

Barygaza. Different categories of textiles may have been for different markets, with finer cotton for export to the Roman world. Coarser cotton garments and sleeping mats may have been personal possessions, and sacking a functional item from the ships (Wild & Wild 2007: 227). Basketry, matting and bamboo, seemingly from North India, were also found at Berenike (Wendrich 2007: 250).

Although *PME* 36 reports the export of teak wood from Barygaza, today, at least, its habitat is not restricted to the north of India and includes peninsular India (Sharma et al. 2002). At Berenike it was imported sometimes as finished objects, but also as planks and boards (occasionally pitched) that could represent remnants of ships or packing crates (Vermeeren 2000: 334-5, 340-1; Van der Veen 2001: 59). The occurrence of wooden brailing rings indicates how the sails were rigged on at least some of the ships (a teak one from Berenike, Vermeeren ibid.; numerous Indian or East African woods at Myos Hormos, Whitewright 2007b: 289). This conforms to known Roman techniques (Wild & Wild 2001: 218), but could equally apply to Indian sails (Whitewright 2007b: 290). The identification of Indian cotton sail-cloth is another important find, strengthened by a fragment attached to a brailing ring at Myos Hormos (Wild & Wild 2001; Handley 2003: 57, fig. 48; Whitewright 2007b: fig. 5). Alternative explanations exist for the planks and sails: Roman-style ships were built in India, Roman ships were repaired in India, or Indian and Roman ships became technologically more similar through time.

Graffiti in Indian languages strongly imply that Indians were living at Red Sea sites. Until recently three Tamil-Brahmi graffiti of personal names had been recovered: two from Myos Hormos and one from Berenike (Mahadevan 1996; Saloman 1991: 734-5). Both date to around the first century AD and provide links with the far south of India where old Tamil was both spoken and written (Mahadevan 1996: 207). Only for the Berenike graffito is the pottery type known, and here it was etched on a Roman amphora of the common Dressel 2-4 type, suggesting that Indians had access to Roman pots. These Indian graffiti are similar to each other and also to ones recorded from Arikamedu (Saloman 1991: 735; Mahadevan 1996: 206-8). More recently a fourth graffito has been identified on an Indian storage jar from Myos Hormos. A double inscription on both sides of the rim reads *paanai oRi,* meaning 'pot (suspended in) a rope net' (Fig. 13 right; Mahadevan 2007). The writing is upside down, so the pot was inverted when it was inscribed suggesting either that it was full but stoppered, or that it was empty. A final written fragment from Myos Hormos dates to the second or third century. Written in Prakrit-Brahmi, a northerly South Indian script, it contains two names that may indicate they were from the Deccan region (Saloman 1991: 731-4). They were very likely merchants: the *ostracon* lists oil, meat and wine, interpreted as personal provisions.

The Indian pottery found in Egypt may also relate to Indian communities, rather than representing trade in ceramics or their contents. This is particularly apt for RW and other fine wares, which are represented by small numbers – *c.* 20 vessels between the two sites. Apart from Myos Hormos and Berenike, the only other sherds of RW known in Egypt are three from the Nile port of Coptos (Elaigne 1999; Reinach 1912). Most of the Indian fine wares from the Red Sea were in contexts of the late first century BC or first century AD. This supports Schenk's revised dating schema, although if strictly applied some sherds were curated before being discarded. Certainly, two sherds from a late first-century BC/early first-century AD context were reworked (Begley & Tomber 1999: cat. nos 4 and 9).

CRSW is much more common, accounting for up to 9% of the

3. Evolution of the Roman Red Sea

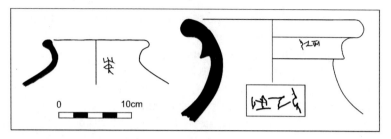

Fig. 13. Graffiti on pottery from Myos Hormos.
Left: Indian jar with a secondary South Arabic monogram.
Right: Tamil-Brahmi secondary graffito incised upside down on the rim of an Indian storage jar.

non-amphora in a first-century AD assemblage from Berenike (ibid.: 180). Representing a variety of sources, at least one from Kerala, they were most common during the Early Roman period and may be residual thereafter. Exceptionally two vessels from Myos Hormos belong to Red-and-Black Megalithic Ware, which predates Early Historic CRSW and hints at pre-Roman contact. Another class of Indian ceramics is the Organic Black Ware from the Gujarat region. Less common than CRSW – although more frequent at Berenike than Myos Hormos – it follows a similar chronology.

Were these wares generally used on-board ship by the crew, or was their primary function as containers for more important items, perhaps holding Indian foodstuffs such as rice, sesame oil or ghee? Although these vessels show no visible sign of having stoppers, in India Early Historic pots were sometimes covered on top and tied with a string that was then secured by a stamped, ceramic seal (Ray 1998: 42), none of which have been identified from Egypt. Apart from a sherd from Vectus Hydreuma, the first road station between Berenike and the Nile, finds of Indian coarse wares are restricted to port sites, indicating that their usage was predominantly for Indians. At Quseir pottery distribution may suggest that foreigners lived or worked in separate quarters (Thomas & Masser 2006: 138).

At Berenike Indian pottery is fairly evenly distributed across the site, mostly from midden deposits rather than primary levels, but South Asian imported basketry clusters in one rubbish dump (Wendrich 2007: 250). A Greek inscription to Pan by a seemingly Hellenised resident Indian found on the caravan route between Berenike and Edfu indicates that Indians travelled in the Eastern Desert and could provide an explanation for the Vectus Hydreuma vessel (Salomon 1991: 735; Sidebotham & Wendrich 2001-2: 29).

Some Indian pottery arrived in Egypt as containers. This is dramatically illustrated by an Indian storage jar at Berenike that contained 7.5 kg of South Indian black pepper. It was found *in situ* in a first-century AD courtyard immediately north of the Serapis temple, the pepper seemingly intended for ritual purposes (Fig. 14; Cappers 2006: 114; in addition, *c.* 3,000 loose peppercorns were retrieved, *c.* 80% charred from ritual use). The jar too is Indian in origin, although an exact source is not known, and suggests that the pepper arrived at Berenike in this container. In general a wide range of Indian storage jars are represented at Berenike and Myos Hormos; the most diagnostic are Paddle Impressed ones that may have originated in eastern India.

Most of the Indian finds present during the Early Roman period – including black pepper – continued into Late Roman times. Although many of the deposits at Berenike had a residual element to them, importantly pepper, Indo-Pacific beads, teak and sapphire also occurred at its satellite site Shenshef (Cappers 2006: 114; Francis 2007: 254; Harrell 1999: 114; Vermeeren 1999). Located 23 km south-south-west of Berenike, the lack of any Early Roman presence demonstrates the continuation of Indian imports into the fifth and early sixth centuries AD. The single Indian coin from the Red Sea coast is a mid- to late fourth-century Kshatrapa coin of Rudrasena III found residually at the Berenike church (Sidebotham 2007:

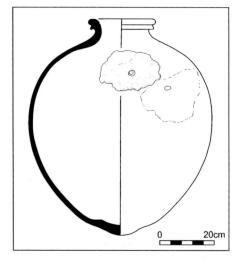

Fig. 14. Indian storage jar from Berenike that contained 7.5 kg of black pepper.

201). For textiles, the Late Roman period saw the addition of resist-dyed cotton and their small number suggests that they may have been personal possessions (Wild & Wild 2000: 272-3). Indian ceramics were less common in the Late Roman period than earlier and they may be residual. If coarse ware importation continued, it was on a much reduced scale.

Turning to East Africa, imports can be identified from proto- and Aksumite times. Some ivory (see above) potentially from this region has been collected from both Berenike and Myos Homos (Hamilton-Dyer 2001: 57; 2002: 67). Pottery, however, is the better sourced import and follows a logical pattern that mirrors the ascendancy of the Aksumite kingdom. Most striking is the distinction between Sandy Red Ware thought to be made north of Adulis and those types that originated in the Aksum region (Aksumite Coarse Wares). At both Myos Hormos and Berenike, Sandy Red Ware cooking pots occurred from the first century AD. They may have arrived from Adulis alongside rare fragments of obsidian sourced to the south side of the Bure Peninsula, Howakil Bay (Peacock et al. 2007: 59; D. Peacock, pers. comm.). Red Sandy Ware seems to have disappeared some time in the third century, while Aksum products – many highly decorated – took over, increasing from the fourth century and continuing into the fifth/early sixth centuries AD at Berenike. Additional handmade fabrics may represent further contact with East Africa, but remain to be studied.

Like the Indian pots, could they have been reserved for an Aksumite community? A Greek *ostracon* from Myos Hormos reading '*Trogodite*', ethnically East African, does little to clarify this question (Tomber 2005b). Other East African finds from Berenike are a graffito with a probable Ethiopic origin from a late fourth-/early fifth-century context (Gragg 1996) and a coin of King Aphilas (*c.* 270/90-before 330 AD) found residually in the church at Berenike (Sidebotham 2007: 201).

A similar range of finds, again dominated by pottery, came from South Arabia. In this case their function is clearer, with large numbers of lined Organic Storage Jars from the Hadramawt, and a much smaller number of Whole-mouth Cooking pots from the region of Aden (Tomber 2004b). Both these types were present during the Early Roman period, but the Organic Storage Jars extended into at least the fourth century (ibid.: 353). An interesting feature of one Organic Storage Jar from Myos Hormos is an incised Greek graffito (Brankaer 2003: 45). Another is a South Arabic monogram scratched on a jar thought to be Indian in origin (Fig. 13 left; Tomber 2004b: fig. 2). Like the Dressel 2-4, these two examples suggest that pottery usage was not restricted within ethnic groups. Also present at Berenike was a primary inscription in Epigraphic South Arabian of the proper name *ydm* (Gragg 1979). A personal glimpse of relations between the Red Sea and South Arabia comes from a papyrus letter to a mother at Berenike from her son returning from Arabia (Sidebotham & Wendrich 2001-2: 41, citing Bagnall & Helms, pers. comm.).

That he has been remiss in writing suggests that he was gone for some period of time.

The Hawdrami Organic Storage Jars may have contained wine, and *PME* 49 lists Arabian wine as an export to India, but not to Egypt. Arabian wine imported into Egypt would have been insignificant in comparison to the trade in frankincense and myrrh. Aromatics do not survive well and residues, for example from incense burners, require scientific analysis for identification. Their trade, however, is indirectly evidenced not only by ceramics, but as Peacock et al. have shown, by unworked basalt that originated from the main frankincense producing areas and reached the Egyptian Red Sea ports as ballast. Of these stones at Myos Hormos, 70% came from Kane/Qana and 30% from Aden (2007: 59). This matches remarkably well with the figures from the pottery, with a greater quantity of Organic Storage Jars from the Hadramawt and small amounts of Whole-mouth Cooking pots from near Aden. From Berenike, basalt from the surface (i.e. undated) was analysed and found to be all from the Hadramawt (Peacock et al. 2007: 59).

Imported finds from Nabataea and Mesopotamia are more likely to relate to overland rather than seaborne trade. During the Early Roman period, a small number of Nabataean fine ware sherds occurred at both Berenike and Myos Hormos, while coarse ware sherds included a single Aila jar at Berenike (not at Myos Hormos, contra Dolinka 2003: 86) and a classic Nabataean cooking pot with a Palmyrene inscription (J. Healey, pers. comm.). Nabataean inscriptions are common throughout the Eastern Desert (Sidebotham 1986: 94) and trade between Nabataea and Rome is well attested.

Mesopotamian finds from the Sasanian and, to a lesser extent, the Parthian period can also be identified. In addition to the Glazed Ware that was found in the earliest deposits at Myos Hormos and during the third and fourth centuries at

Berenike (Fig. 10), was a Sasanian cameo decorated with the symbol for a Zoroastrian fire altar (Francis 2000: 223).

The Parthians and Sasanians ranked as Rome and Byzantium's most enduring rivals. Mesopotamian finds most likely arrived indirectly via the Palmyrenes, whose presence in the Eastern Desert both as merchants and military personnel is well documented. In fact, an association of Palmyrene merchants – 'Palmyrene Red Sea Shipowners' – lived at Coptos (Sidebotham 1986: 95-6; Casson 1989: 34). Two Palmyrene inscriptions have been excavated at Berenike. The first, dated to 8 September 215 AD, is a dedication in Greek by a Palmyrene archer to the emperor Caracalla (Verhoogt 1998). The second comprises a partial bilingual dedication in Palmyrene and Greek dating to the late second or the early third century (Dijkstra & Verhoogt 1999).

At Aila non-Roman imports differ dramatically from those at Berenike and Myos Hormos, both in range and quantity. From South Arabia there is only one sherd of an Organic Storage Jar in a fourth-century context (Tomber 2004b: 353). There are, instead, fragments of steatite bowls also thought to be from Yemen that occurred from the fourth century into the Islamic period, when they were common (Parker 1998: 389).

East African pottery is much sparser than at Myos Hormos and Berenike: apparently the Red Sandy Ware was absent and only approximately a dozen Aksumite sherds could be identified. Of these, half came from Late Roman deposits, the remainder from Early Islamic ones. There are, however, two Aksumite coins from excavated deposits: one late fourth- or fifth-century, the other from the seventh or early eighth (Whitcomb 1994: 16-18) or second half of the sixth century (Hahn 2000: 286).

Despite ancient texts stressing Aila's role in trade with India (Procopius *History of the Wars* 1.19.24 and above) Indian pottery is rare, represented by one sherd of Organic Black

Ware from a late fourth-/fifth-century context. Textual references to 'India' may therefore denote Ethiopia, but Aksumite pottery, too, is less numerous at Aila than at Berenike. Approximately 40 sherds of non-Roman handmade pottery were recovered from the first five seasons, but with few diagnostic sherds it is difficult to assign them to a source area, and so Indian and Aksumite sources may be under-represented. Nor have any Indian or Asian plant remains been identified from Aila, although only a small percentage of the samples collected have as yet been analysed (Ramsay 2006).

Thus far the emphasis has been on finds imported from beyond the Roman world, but clear distinctions also exist between Aila and Myos Hormos/Berenike in terms of Roman ceramics. The Egyptian sites exhibit a range of imported pottery from throughout the Roman world – essentially everything that was available in Alexandria was found along the Egyptian Red Sea coast in varying amounts. At Berenike the custom passes commonly mention Italian wine amphorae – *italika* – to be loaded onto ships (Bagnall et al. 2000: 16-21). Certainly Italian Dressel 2-4 amphorae are the most common Early Roman imported type at both Berenike and Myos Hormos. The custom passes tend to be for relatively small quantities, averaging around eight amphorae per pass, the largest for 48. These are not quantities one might associate with either Roman or Indian sea-going vessels with estimated capacities in the thousands (Parker 1992: 26; Ray 1996: 361; *NH* 6.83). The passes could have been for small-scale merchants or larger shipments that had been broken down for transport (Bagnall et al. 2000: 14-16). Some amphorae may have been used on the voyage, and one *ostracon* that details the reuse of a foreign amphora for local (i.e. Egyptian) wine (ibid.: 18, fig. 1) could have served this purpose.

At Myos Hormos a certain Miresis is inscribed on a Dressel

2-4 from Cilicia. The name is rare, but belongs to one of Nicanor's sons, active between AD 41 and 62 (Van Rengen 2003: 43). In addition to Miresis, other names link Berenike, Myos Hormos and the Nicanor archive: a papyrus from Myos Hormos mentions Agathopus, known, from a receipt probably from the Nicanor archive, as an agent of Publius Mamilius Chresimus from Coptos *c.* 18 BC (Van Rengen 2002: 53).

In contrast, Aila has a more restricted range of Mediterranean amphorae, with the most common types from Gaza and, from the Late Roman period, Egypt (S.T. Parker 2002: 424-5). Other Mediterranean amphorae are rare, although fine wares are common, particularly ESA during the early period and Tunisian African Red Slip Ware (ARS) during the late. Aila probably received its amphorae via Clysma or Gaza rather than from Myos Hormos or Berenike. Little is known about the assemblages from Clysma or Gaza, although on the basis of illustrated vessels it seems Egyptian amphorae dominated at Clysma alongside some Early Roman potential imports (Bruyère 1966: pl. xxiv).

Table 1. Non-Roman imported finds represented archaeologically at Myos Hormos, Berenike and Aila. (ER = Early Roman; LR = Late Roman); *West India refers to the north-west area of peninsular India. Natural sources for gems refer to those most commonly thought to be exploited in Antiquity. (Modified from Wendrich et al. 2003: tables 1-2).

| Product | Suggested Source *Periplus port for export* | ER Myos Hormos | ER Berenike | LR/Other Berenike & Shenshef | LR/Other Aila |
|---|---|---|---|---|---|
| **Food** | | | | | |
| Rice | India *Barygaza, Limyrike* | ✓ | ✓ | ✓ | |
| Black pepper | India (SW) *Limyrike* | ✓ | ✓ | ✓ | |
| Coconut | India | ✓ | ✓ | ✓ | |
| Emblic | India/Sri Lanka | | ✓ | | |
| Mung bean | India/Sri Lanka | | ✓ | | |
| Abrus | East Africa? | | ✓ | ✓ | |
| Abyssinian pea | Ethiopia | | ✓ | ✓ | |
| Baobab | East Africa | | | ✓ | |
| Tamarind | East Africa | | ✓ | | |
| **Wood and ivory** | | | | | |
| Teak | India *Barygaza* | ✓ | ✓ | ✓ | |
| Rhodesian teak | Africa | | ✓ | ✓ | |
| Bamboo | India | | | ✓ | |
| Sandalwood | India/Mediterranean | | ✓ | | |
| Ivory | Africa/India/Arabia *Many ports, especially Adulis* | ✓ | ✓ | ✓ | |

Table 1 continued

| Product | Suggested Source *Periplus port for export* | ER Myos Hormos | ER Berenike | LR/Other Berenike & Shenshef | LR/Othert Aila |
|---|---|---|---|---|---|
| **Textiles and basketry** | | | | | |
| Cotton | India *Barbarikon, Barygaza, Limyrike, Ganges* | ✓ | ✓ | ✓ | |
| Cotton, resist dye | India | ✓ Islamic? | | ✓ | |
| Cotton, sail cloth | India | ✓ | ✓ | ✓ | |
| Basketry/matting | India (North) | | ✓ | | |
| **Epigraphy and coins** | | | | | |
| Graffito | Prakrit-Brahmi | ✓ | | | |
| Graffiti | Tamil-Brahmi | ✓ | ✓ | | |
| Graffiti | South Arabian | ✓ | | | ✓ modern context |
| Graffiti | Ethiopic | ✓ | ✓ | ✓ | |
| Graffiti/inscriptions | Palmyrene | ✓ | | | |
| Coin | India (West*) | | | ✓ | |
| Coins | Aksum | | | ✓ | ✓ |

Table 1 continued

| Product | Suggested Source<br>*Periplus port for export* | ER<br>Myos Hormos | ER<br>Berenike | LR/Other<br>Berenike & Shenshef | LR/Other<br>Aila |
|---|---|---|---|---|---|
| **Gems** | | | | | |
| Agate, onyx, sardonyx (banded variety of quartz.) | India (West*)<br>*Barygaza* | | ✓ | ✓ | |
| Carnelian and sard (red and brown varieties of quartz) | India (West*/South?)/Egypt | | ✓ | ✓ | |
| Almandine garnet | India (South)<br>*Limryike (PME 56 transparent gems)* | | ✓ | ✓ | |
| Rock crystal (colourless variety of quartz) | India (South)<br>*Limryike (PME 56 transparent gems)* | | ✓ | ✓ | |
| Amethyst (purple variety of quartz) | India (South)/Egypt<br>*Limryke (PME 56 transparent gems)* | | ✓ | ✓ | |
| Aquamarine (variety of beryl) | India (South)<br>*Limryke (PME 56 transparent gems)* | | ✓ | ✓ | |
| Emerald (variety of beryl) | India (South)/Egypt<br>*Limryke (PME 56 transparent gems)* | | ✓ | ✓ | |
| Sapphire (variety of corundum) | Sri Lanka<br>*Limryke (PME 56 transparent gems)* | | ✓ | ✓ | |
| Lapis lazuli | Afghanistan (NE)<br>*Barbarikon* | | ✓ | | |

85

Table 1 continued

| Product | Suggested source<br>*Periplus port for export* | ER<br>Myos Hormos | ER<br>Berenike | LR/Other<br>Berenike & Shenshef | LR/Other<br>Aila |
|---|---|---|---|---|---|
| **Rocks** | | | | | |
| Basalt | Hadramawt | ✓ | | ✓ surface | |
| Basalt | Aden | ✓ | | | |
| Calcite jars | Arabia (SW?) | ✓ | | ✓ | |
| Steatite bowls | Yemen | | | | ✓ |
| Obsidian | Eritrea<br>*Howakil Bay* | ✓ | ✓ | ✓ | |
| | | | | | |
| **Beads and ornaments** | | | | | |
| Mosaic bead | Java | | | ✓ surface | |
| Indo-Pacific glass beads | South India/Sri Lanka | | ✓ | ✓ | |
| Pearls | Gulf/India (Gulf of Mannar)<br>*Limyrike, Gange, Omana* | | ✓ | | |
| Ostrich egg bead | East Africa | | | ✓ | |
| Job's tear beads | India (East/NE) | | ✓ | ✓ | |
| Glass cameo | Sasanian | | | ✓ surface | |

Table 1 continued

| Product | Suggested Source<br>*Periplus port for export* | ER<br>Myos Hormos | ER<br>Berenike | LR/Other<br>Berenike & Shenshef | LR/Other<br>Aila |
|---|---|---|---|---|---|
| **Pottery** | | | | | |
| Glazed Ware | Mesopotamia | ✓ | ? | ✓ | |
| RW & related | India (NE) | ✓ | ✓ | ✓ residual? | |
| CRSW | India (including SW) | ✓ | ✓ | ✓ residual? | |
| Paddle Impressed Wares | India (East?) | ✓ | ✓ | ✓ residual? | |
| Coarse Wares | India | ✓ | ✓ | ✓ residual? | |
| Organic Black Ware | India (NW) | ✓ | ✓ | ✓ residual? | ✓ residual? |
| Organic Storage Jars | Hadramawt | ✓ | ✓ | ✓ | ✓ |
| Whole-mouth Cooking pot | South Arabia (Aden) | ✓ | ✓ | | |
| Red Sandy Ware | Adulis region | ✓ | ✓ | ✓ residual? | |
| Coarse Wares | Aksum region | ✓ | ? | ✓ | ✓ |

# 4

# Beyond the Roman world

## Africa's role in Indian Ocean trade

The *Periplus* defines a region of Barbaroi, incorporating parts of modern Egypt south of Berenike and the coastal regions east of the Nile in Sudan, Ethiopia, Eritrea and Somalia (Casson 1989: fig. 2). The African ports are often considered to be on a separate route from the Red Sea-India or Arabia-India ones (ibid.: 34, 283), and this is further discussed in Chapter 6. At this time Aksum exerted strong political control over South Arabia, which would have expedited trade relations between the regions.

### *Powerful partners: the Aksumite kingdom and its port* (Figs 15-16)

Between the third and seventh centuries AD the Aksumites were a powerful international force. Although their capital Aksum, in modern Ethiopia, was landlocked, they played an active role in Indian Ocean commerce through their port of Adulis, *c.* 150 km to the north-east in Eritrea. They are generally considered to have been more important to overseas commerce than the Romans during this period, acting as their middlemen (Sidebotham 1986: 46-7). For this period, Cosmas Indicopleustes' writings are most relevant, describing first-hand his travels to Adulis, Aksum and further inland (*Topography* 2.48-57). His *Christian Topography* also transcribed the *Monumentum Adulitanum*, which includes an enigmatic

## 4. Beyond the Roman world

Greek inscription now thought to have been written by a Himyarite king (see below) describing the incorporation of Ethiopia and the Hadramawt into his kingdom (*Topography* 2.60-3; Kirwan 1972: 171-6). Just when this occurred has been much debated, but a date in the mid-third century is most likely (Munro-Hay 1991: 79-80; Robin 1981).

Even before the third century the Aksumites belonged to an international trading network via Adulis. *PME* 4 clearly notes the importance of Adulis, eight days distant from Aksum, particularly for the export of ivory from the interior and tortoiseshell from coastal areas. Neither of these products can be readily sourced, which makes tracking exports difficult. The *Periplus* describes Adulis as being situated 20 *stadia* from the coast with the actual port facilities found on Oriene Island within a bay, furthermore stating that the port had previously been located at the furthest mainland point of the bay, at Didoros Island.

The accepted location for Adulis was first identified by Henry Salt in 1810 by its extensive ruins, and excavations by the British Museum took place in 1868 (Munro-Hay 1989b). Subsequent exploration focused on the same location and revealed a thriving urban centre during the Late Roman or Byzantine period (Paribeni 1907; Littmann 1913; Sundström 1907; Anfray 1974). Extensive architecture included a monumental building interpreted by the excavator as a palace (Sundström 1907: 178) and three churches (Munro-Hay 1982: 108, 1989b; Paribeni 1907) that demonstrate the importance of Christianity in the region, officially converted by *c.* AD 340. An earlier supposedly archaic phase was also identified by Paribeni, but no imported finds relating to the time of the *Periplus* were published. However, survey work in 2004 and 2005, conducted by David Peacock and Lucy Blue, has resolved this longstanding inconsistency: they identified probable locations for Oriene and Diodoros Islands with associated

Early Roman pottery. Their finds from the ruins at Adulis itself reinforce the Late Roman date, *c.* fifth-seventh century (2007: 37, 56-64). Furthermore, in the south-west corner of the site four $^{14}$C dates were taken from shells associated with some early local pottery. Calibrated, these dates range between 10 BC and AD 360, and indicate that this area of the site was active during the time of the *Periplus* (Peacock 2007a: 93). According to Casson's edition, *PME* 6 reports that 'a little Roman money for the resident foreigners' was imported to Adulis (Casson 1989: 19, 53); Schoff, instead, refers only to 'a little coin for those coming to the market' (1912: 24).

Aksum, the capital of the kingdom, has also been extensively investigated and in addition to field reports is covered in other works more broadly concerned with Aksumite history and culture (Munro-Hay 1991; Phillipson 1998). Explored by the Deutsche-Aksum Expedition in 1906 as part of a broader survey of the region (Littman 1913), the site has more recently been investigated by numerous Ethiopian and European teams from its prehistoric (pre-Aksumite) to its medieval sequence. Strong links with South Arabia existed from the pre-Akusmite period, while in the proto-Aksumite those with the Nile Valley were also pronounced (Philippson 2000: 474-5, 482). Chittick's 1970s excavation reported on by Munro-Hay (1989c; Chittick 1974) was a landmark in the understanding of Aksum, as are Phillipson's excavations at a number of sites throughout Aksum, including monumental stelae marking burials and their associated areas (2000). Italian teams, too, have had an ongoing presence, focused on Bieta Giyorgis, 1 km north-west of Aksum. Ricci and Fattovich's (1987) excavations included a basilica church and those by Fattovich and Bard a cemetery dated between the first century BC and fourth century AD (e.g. Bard et al. 1997: 389-92).

Imported finds from Adulis and Aksum are biased towards the fifth to seventh centuries and include a range of pottery, glass and jewellery (Munro-Hay 1991; Paribeni 1907; Manzo 2005; Peacock & Blue 2007; Phillips 2000; Philippson 2000; Williams 2000). Additional Roman evidence comes from a coin of Valerian (AD 253-60) from Adulis (Paribeni 1907: fig. 11). Other finds have an Egyptian source, particularly an Abu Mena flask (ibid.: fig. 54) made in the vicinity of Alexandria and a faience or glass scarab of uncertain date (ibid.: fig. 3). Both may have arrived as personal possessions via the Nile or the Red Sea. Aqaba amphorae certainly arrived via the Red Sea and are the most common amphorae at Aksum, and also at Adulis where some were reused (Munro-Hay 1991: 235). Small quantities of Eastern Mediterranean amphorae (LR1 and LR3) and ARS are present at both sites. Here, however, they diverge: at Adulis LR2 and North African amphorae are also present, where with the other non-Aqaba amphorae they account for only *c.* 2% (D. Peacock, pers. comm.). Mesopotamian Glazed Ware points to a different sea route originating in the Gulf.

The glass assemblage at Aksum is exceptional in quantity and quality. Although some imported vessels were found, glass may have been locally produced or at least worked (Morrison 1989: 209; Harlow 2000: 459; Manzo 2005: 59). The late fourth-century Tomb of the Brick Arches is particularly rich and includes imports from the Eastern Roman Empire (Harlow ibid.). The vessels from this tomb and many of the other Aksum finds are from non-domestic, high status features. A similar pattern is seen in the range of Roman decorative stone from Turkey, Greece, France and possibly Egypt imported to Adulis (Peacock 2007b: 115). The elite distribution of finds at Aksum suggests to Manzo a degree of state-controlled trade (2005: 63).

Early Roman imports are less common and come mostly from Bieta Giyorgis. Again glass (including millefiore) is regularly identified, but amphorae are sparse and *sigillata* even more so (ESB?, De Conteson 1963: pl. xxf; Manzo 2005: fig. 21 for an overview). A rare find is a South Gaulish amphora with the maker's mark <MATUR> (Fattovich & Bard 1995: figs 2-4) of the potter Maturus (Laubenheimer 1985: 429, fig. 201, no. 30). In this period, several Meroitic vessels (Fattovich & Bard 1993: 17) may reinforce a Nile route for some imports. As noted above, the Adulis Early Roman finds are sparse, but include a number of Dressel 2-4 wine amphorae, some from Campania, and *sigillata* from Syria and possibly Italy (Peacock 2007a: 79-83).

Off-shore from Adulis, the shipwreck of the Black Assarca between Dahlak Kabir and the coastline also belongs to the Late Roman period and includes amphora types found at Adulis and Aksum. Pedersen recorded two main pottery types: Aqaba amphorae and costrels or flasks, which are reported as having a similarly coloured fabric to the amphorae (2000: 5). The identification of Aqaba costrels at Adulis (Peacock 2007a: 97, fig. 8.16, no. 4) lends weight to this interpretation and suggests that the cargo was assembled at Aila. Another vessel type, identified from photos, is LR1 (Pedersen 2000: fig. 9). A date between the fifth and mid-seventh century is likely.

Late Roman finds similar to those found at Adulis and Aksum were also recovered from Matara, an urban site with monumental public buildings (including churches), tombs and some domestic structures. Excavated by the French in the 1960s, Roman fine wares and Mesopotamian Glazed Ware were identified, as were Aqaba amphorae reused as water pipes or infant coffins (Anfray 1974: 752, 757-8, 1966) and a glass head flask (Morrison 1989: 195). Most spectacular was a cache of gold Roman coins dating primarily to the Antonine period and reused as pendants on a necklace (Anfray & Annequin 1965: 68, pl. lxix, figs 3-4). Elsewhere in the region Roman coins are rare and only one other is known. This is a coin of Constantine from Qohayto (Munro-Hay 1982: 111), thought to be Koloe, the staging post between Adulis and Aksum (*PME* 4; Raunig 2004). As shown in Figs 15-16, Aqaba

4. Beyond the Roman world

amphorae have been recorded at other sites in the region, but it is difficult to verify the identification of unillustrated examples.

The increased number of late, compared to early, Roman finds from Adulis and Aksum supports the premise of greater Aksumite involvement during this period. Since Aqaba amphorae form the bulk of these finds, a seaborne route is fairly assured. From Cosmas (*Topography* 2.54) we also learn that traders from Aila (and Alexandria) visited Adulis. Some of the imports to Aksum may have arrived via the Nile, which further reduces the role of an early sea route.

The lack of ceramic and botanical remains from India is in sharp contrast to that seen from sites on the Egyptian Red Sea. This is surprising if Aksumites or Indians were active in this leg of the trade. Beads likely to originate in India are an exception and occurred in great numbers: of the 1,139 beads from the Tomb of the Brick Arches there are 163 biconical faceted and 883 of the small Indo-Pacific beads (Harlow 2000: 83-6), which seem also to be found at Matara (Anfray & Annequin 1965: pl. clv b, top row). In any case, a cosmopolitan milieu is apparent at Aksum from classically inspired ivory furniture and figurines and a metal plaque with Chinese or East Asian inspiration (Phillipson 2000: 115, 118-19, 123, figs 95-6, 97-8, 105). From Adulis, Kobishanov suggested that a gold and carnelian ring inscribed in an unknown language might be Indian (1979: 174; Paribeni 1907: fig. 49). A hoard of gold Kushana coins dating to *c.* AD 220 was found at Debra Damo (Munro-Hay 1991: 182), although in a sixth-century context (Finneran 2007: 204).

### Through the Bab al-Mandab (Fig. 15)

To reach Somalia and South Arabia for frankincense and myrrh – immensely important in the Roman world – the first hurdle was through the Bab al-Mandab, sailing along the Gulf

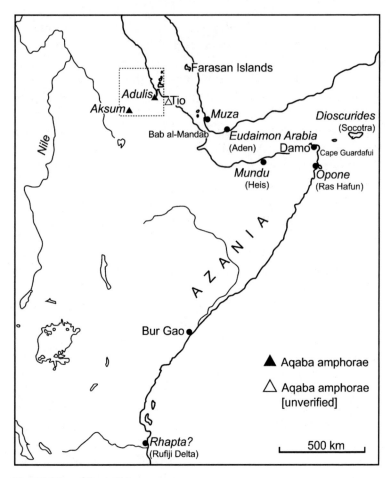

Fig. 15. Map of East Africa.

of Aden to Cape Guardafui. This area of coastline, in modern Somalia, was subject to the same broad sailing regimes as the Red Sea (J. Whitewright, pers. comm.; Whitewright 2007), with conditions improving as ships turned south and travelled down the east coast of Africa. It is only on this northern coast, of the 'Far Side Barbaria' that the writer of the *Periplus* recognises the

94

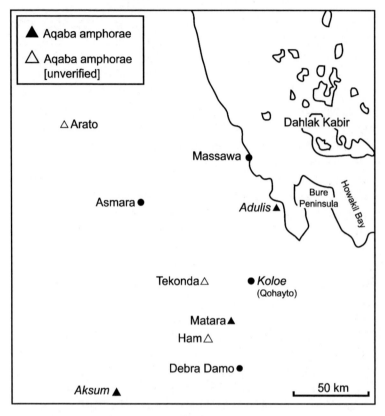

Fig. 16. Detailed map of the Adulis-Aksum region.

occasional trade practice of tramping along the coast (*PME* 14). The *Trogodites* dwelled here and from north-west Somalia came the finest myrrh of all, sometimes known as '*Trogoditic* myrrh' (Pliny *NH* 12.69; *PME* 7, Casson 1989: 120). Here too South Arabian connections were strong, for during the time of the *Periplus* Azania was under their control (*PME* 16).

Along the Far Side coast, Classical remains have been recorded from Heis and Damo. Those from Heis result from the nineteenth-century excavations of burial mounds by Révoil

(1882). Heis itself is frequently equated with Mundu of the *Periplus* (*PME* 9; Casson 1989: 126-7; Chittick 1979: 274). The material collected by Révoil is particularly informative since it has recently been assessed and broadly conforms to the time of the *Periplus*. Ballet has assigned sources to eight of nine fine ware vessels, including *sigillata* from Italy and Syria and Egyptian faience, as well as a Campanian Dressel 2-4 wine amphora and an alabaster vase, possibly Egyptian (Ballet 1993, 1996: 823). Stern recorded over 100 glass fragments, many for inlay, as well as 11 vessels; mosaic glass is common and of probable Egyptian origin (*PME* 6; Stern 1993). Chittick suggested that this rich glass assemblage – its import is mentioned in *PME* 9 – was intended as burial goods (Chittick 1979: 275).

Further west on Cape Guardafui is Damo, where Chittick found what he identified as Parthian Glazed Ware and amphora handles in an area disturbed by quarrying; potential rock-cut building foundations were also reported (Chittick 1976: 123-4). His amphora identifications were subsequently refined to Campanian Dressel 2-4s by Ballet (1993: 66). Damo may be the Spice Port of the *Periplus* (*PME* 12; Casson 1989: 129).

South of Cape Guardafui is Ras Hafun, long equated with Opone (*PME* 13; ibid.: 132). Chittick identified the site as part of a wider survey of Somalia and subsequently returned there to excavate Hafun West (HW) and, slightly to the south-east, Hafun Main (HM) (1976). The ceramics have been published by Smith and Wright, who suggested that Opone was located somewhere nearby and that these two sites represent beach camps related to the emporium (1988: 138). The promontory suffers from harsh monsoon winds between November and March, but protects the sites (ibid.: 116, fig. 2). Structurally little remains of either, but the ceramics comprise the most substantial assemblages from this region, mostly from HM. At HW there was a building complex heavily eroded by water leaving stone footings visible. HM was undisturbed, but lacked architectural features, apart from a few rock-cut cairns.

Smith and Wright dated the pottery from HW to the first century BC/AD and drew attention to two main facets: first a Mediterranean-style group with an important Egyptian component and second Glazed Ware and jars that reached the site via the Gulf (ibid.: fig. 5, nos a-c). From HM they distinguished assemblages of the second-third and third-fifth centuries AD. It is now clear that neither of the HM assemblages had a Mediterranean element, but both had common Glazed Ware, Torpedo jars and other wares potentially from the Gulf (ibid.: fig. 7, nos a-b, l-m, fig. 9, nos a-g; Kennet 2004: 58, 63) . In 1988 the South Asian elements were difficult to identify, but the authors tentatively identified rare sherds at HW that increased in the early phase of HM and were severely reduced or absent from the latest levels (Smith & Wright 1988: 124-5, 138). Recent studies enable more South Asian wares to be identified and show they were somewhat more common at HW and the early phases of HM than originally thought, although this does not alter Smith and Wright's overall conclusions (ibid.: at least fig. 4, nos f-g, fig. 6, nos a-c; possibly fig. 8, nos a-e). Organic Black Ware, sourced to North India, has now been identified from the early phase of HM (ibid.: fig. 8, nos h-j). Unidentified materials are represented at both sites that could include Ethiopian sources.

Azania, the remaining coast covered by the *Periplus* (*PME* 15-17), extends from Opone to Rhapta and has been mistakenly associated with the trade in cinnamon and *cassia* (Chapter 2, pp. 54-5). From Opone southwards, archaeological evidence becomes more ephemeral and the identification of sites more controversial, complicated by discrepancies between the *Periplus* and Ptolemy (Datoo 1970; Kirwan 1986; Casson 1989: 141). Rhapta is described as a port of trade in the *Periplus* (*PME* 16) and as a metropolis in Ptolemy (*Geography* 4.7.12), which is frequently taken as a measure of its growing importance from the mid-first to the mid-second century. Overall Ptolemy presents a more detailed description of the East African coast and if one credits his observations to the mid-second century, this may reflect economic development of this region or at least increased Greco-Roman participation.

The recognition of *Periplus* sites in Azania has been hindered by the lack of reliable Classical period finds, although there was intense activity during the Islamic period. Horton has summarised the occurrence of foreign coins collected from Tanzania/Zanzibar, Kenya, South Africa, Zimbabwe and Uganda (1996: 446-8). Diverse sources are represented, including Roman, Parthian and from Zimbabwe even Indian coins. Most groups are mixed in date and the circumstance of their discovery is in doubt, therefore their value in documenting Indian Ocean commerce is limited. The best known hoard comes from Bur Gao on the southern Somalian coast. Over 100 coins were found in 1912; they are primarily fourth-century, but their range between the Ptolemaic period and eighteenth century makes the integrity of even this group questionable (Mattingly 1932).

Extensive work by Chami in Tanzania and its off-shore islands has uncovered a tantalising range of pottery and beads (including a gold foil one) of possible Roman and Indian origin (1999, 2002, 2004). On the basis of finds, Chami has placed Rhapta in the Rufiji Delta, and while further exploration is needed, to date it is the most convincing location. Nevertheless, the finds from this region are difficult to source and date (Sinclair 2007) and at present add little to an overall account. Gold foil beads provide markers of the Classical world, but the growing recognition of bead manufacture in Asia (e.g. Lankton & Dussubieux 2006) could alter this assumption in future. From Zanzibar come two potentially Egyptian sherds from fifth- or sixth-century levels (Juma 1996), although the stabbing marks on Pot B are unusual for Egyptian wares. Chami's ongoing work is important to achieve a better understanding of this coastline.

The range of Roman finds from Heis, Damo and Hafun West provides strong evidence for contact with the Roman world during the time of the *Periplus*. At Heis and Damo the preponderance of fine wares over amphorae, together with the glass, highlights a non-utilitarian strand of exchange. The quantity, however, could be explained by a single shipload. *PME* 13 states that goods, including *cassia*, were sent to Egypt from Opone and this offers a ready explanation for both Roman and Indian (a true source of *cassia*) pottery at Hafun.

Smith and Wright saw the mixed nature of both Hafun assemblages as resulting from ports recently visited for provisions, rather than reflecting the ethnicity of the traders (1988: 138). Salles has argued that beyond Cape Guardafui the route was monopolised by Arabs from Muza (1993: 506-7), but other routes between Africa and the Red Sea or between Persia and Africa also appear to have been active. The finds at Hafun can be seen to reflect the terminus for several different voyages to HW. In terms of quantity, direct trips from the Red Sea and another via the Gulf seem likely; a direct route from India is not ruled out but is less likely to account for the small number of Asian finds. In what direction these voyages were undertaken could be assessed better with the identification of Somalian pottery and whether it occurs in Egypt, South Arabia or elsewhere.

Thereafter, a dramatic change occurred. Only Hafun Main was active during the Late Roman period, although significantly only to the fifth century. The lack of Late Roman finds at HM suggests that relations with the Romans had ceased, and that Adulis now provided the meeting place for foreign traders. Connections with India were strongest during the second/third century and they too may have ceased during the fifth century.

By this time the route was dominated by the Gulf, reflecting the rise in Sasanian power (Smith & Wright 1988: 140).

## Arabia Felix (Fig. 17)

The *Periplus* devotes most of 12 sections to Arabia (*PME* 20-32). Although South Arabia was never under Roman rule, Augustus attempted to subdue the eastern side of the Red Sea through the campaign of L. Aelius Gallus (25-24 BC). A military inscription of AD 143-4 has recently been published by Phillips et al. (2004). Found on the Farasan Islands, it hints at the presence of a *vexillation* of the *Legio II* there. *Legio II* was stationed in Egypt and probably sailed from Berenike, suggesting more Roman involvement in the region than has been previously documented. Indirectly, however, Augustus and Roman policy had a profound effect on the demography of Arabia, for the harnessing of the monsoons and the annexation of Egypt shifted the emphasis of Eastern trade to a sea-borne one at the expense of the existing caravan routes (Hoyland 2003: 42-5).

From earliest times, though, South Arabia had closer ties with East Africa than the Roman world. The history of the incense lands – Arabia Felix to the Romans (Arabia Eudaimon to the Greeks) or essentially pre-Islamic Yemen – is one of the rise and fall of politically separate kingdoms (Hoyland 2002: 70-2, 2003: 40-57; Singer 2007: 10-13). Four main kingdoms were involved in the overland incense trade: Saba, Hadramawt, Qataban and Ma, with their respective capitals at Marib, Shabwa, Timna and Qarnaw. By the time of the *Periplus* and the establishment of seaborne routes, the Himyarites and Sabaeans were the most powerful and together ruled not only South Arabia but most of Azania (*PME* 23; Hoyland 2002: 71-2). Gradual shifts changed the political landscape so that by the late second century Qataban was

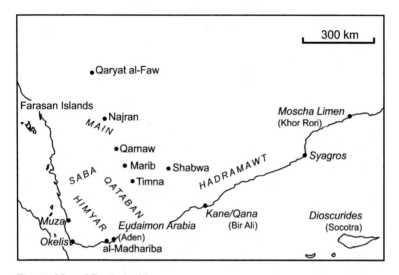

Fig. 17. Map of South Arabia.

annexed by Hadramawt and Himyar, and by the late third century AD the Himyarites had unified South Arabia. Around and slightly after AD 300, external relations became paramount and Arabian embassies were sent to Persia and Ethiopia; from the Roman world an embassy was sent to Arabia that promoted the construction of churches for merchants visiting Himyar. By the sixth century there was an Ethiopic presence in South Arabia that continued until a Persian intervention in the mid-sixth century; thereafter Ethiopia or Persia controlled South Arabia until the Muslim takeover in AD 628. According to Cosmas, the Himyarites served as middlemen for the Romans in the sixth century (Mango 1996: 154; *Topography* 2.49-50).

Of the export items, myrrh and frankincense, synonymous with the region, were the most sought after aromatics and commanded the highest prices, particularly frankincense. The aromatics trade was established by the eighth century BC and progressively flourished. It followed not one but a number of

101

caravan routes with goods destined for the Mediterranean travelling through Nabataean controlled areas and eventually funnelled through Gaza, as described by Groom (1981: chs 9-10) and Singer (2007: 11-18). In the early centuries AD the overland trade continued in tandem with the seaborne one, and sites such as Qana and Timna contributed to both networks. Thus, at least during the Early Roman period, Mediterranean goods may have reached South Arabia by either land or sea routes; occasionally one can separate them from each other. The presence of Nabataean pottery at sites such as Marib (Stucky 1983: Abb. 10-11), Qaryat al-Faw (al-Ansary 1982: 22, figs 2-3), Khor Rori (Sedov & Benvenuti 2002: 192) and Qana (Sedov 1992: 120), and Nabataean inscriptions found as part of a broad epigraphic survey in Saudi Arabia (e.g. al-Kabawi et al.1989) attest to overland travel.

For the sea trade the *Periplus* names Muza, Okelis, Eudaimon Arabia, Kane, Syagros and Moscha Limen. Of these only Muza, Kane/Qana and Moscha are described as ports and only Qana and Moscha, established when the incense trade began to shift from overland to seaborne routes, are known archaeologically. We will focus on them, but first the village of Eudaimon Arabia warrants mention. *PME* 26 describes it as an important trans-shipment point between India and the West prior to the *Periplus*:

> ... since vessels from India did not go on to Egypt and those from Egypt did not dare sail to the places further on but came only this far, it used to receive the cargoes of both ...

Despite the lack of archaeological evidence, Eudaimon Arabia is generally considered to be located at Aden (Casson 1989: 158-9); basalt (Peacock et al. 2007: 59) and pottery (Tomber 2004b: 356) seemingly exported from this area lend support to this location. It is possible that by the time of Ptolemy, a hundred years later, Eudaimon Arabia may have regained its importance (Casson 1989: 159). Recently pre-Islamic finds, particularly from graves, have been reported from the area and more systematic work may well locate it on the ground (Sedov 2007: 98). At al-Madhariba, 70 km west of Aden, a hoard of Roman (326) and Aksumite (868) coins dated between the mid-fourth and mid-sixth century AD has been found (Munro-Hay 1989a).

Kane/Qana (Bir Ali, Yemen) and Moscha Limen (Khor Rori, Oman) were also vital points in the incense trade. Qana was first seen by Europeans in 1834, who described a large rock, Husn al-Gurab, with a fortress on top and a large settlement at its foot. The building at the highest point, excavated in 1972, was identified as a lighthouse. The ancient settlement or 'Lower City' was excavated by a Soviet-Yemeni team between 1985 and 1991 and the most recent synthesis of the three periods (Lower, Middle and Upper) and their finds is summarised by Sedov (2007).

Although some consider Qana to have been occupied during biblical times, the earliest excavated period (Lower) comprised a building at the base of Husn al-Gurab dated between the mid-first century BC and the late first century AD. Its function as an incense warehouse was graphically demonstrated by a destruction deposit that included burnt frankincense. *PME* 27-8 describes Qana as an important collecting and distribution point for frankincense.

In the Middle period, between the second and fifth centuries, occupation was at its most intensive and numerous buildings – domestic, commercial and religious – were occupied, although instead of a large warehouse, storage was in smaller units. A cemetery was established, and a wall defended access to the hill. Religious structures included those for local and Jewish worship. Qana was now the major port for the Hadramawt and subsequently Himyarite kingdoms. By the sixth century, the Upper period, occupation had declined, consisting primarily of burials and domestic structures that were gradually abandoned by the early seventh century.

The site dating relies primarily on South Arabian coinage and imported pottery, which comprises up to 75% of the ceramics. The assemblage is rich and diverse with sources from the Roman world, East Africa, India and Mesopotamia all well represented (Sedov 2007: 76-90; Sedov 1998; Ballet 1996: 823-8). The Lower period was dominated by Roman wares, including amphorae from Campania, Rhodes, the Aegean, Spain and Egypt, Egyptian coarse wares, and fine wares from Italy, Syria, Egypt and Nabataea. Underwater assemblages from Qana supplement the corpus of Early Roman pottery types with additional coarse wares from Egypt and Indian vessels identified (Davidde et al. 2004). All of the Roman types were available at Alexandria, Myos Hormos and Berenike; rare Nabataean wares could also indicate a route from Aila or Leuke Kome. A sea itinerary would account for Indian and Mesopotamian pottery.

During the Middle period, Roman pottery decreased and mirrored changes in Roman trade in general, with North African sources important. Indian storage jars and cooking pots and Mesopotamian sources were more common, and Hadrami types decreased. Sedov sees this as a shift in function from a small port serving boats between Qana and Egypt, to a major Hadrami port for Indian Ocean commerce (2007: 104-5). In the latest levels of the Middle period, Aksumite wares first occurred, as did lined storage jars, published as Palestinian (ibid.: fig. 4.16), which could well be Mesopotamian Torpedo jars. These later levels of the Middle period probably equate more with a Late Roman than an Early Roman horizon.

By the Upper horizon, Roman finds shifted from Western to Eastern Mediterranean sources, particularly Levantine ones.

## 4. Beyond the Roman world

Gaza and Aqaba amphorae probably arrived together directly down the Red Sea from Aila. Torpedo jars (published as LR4, Sedov 2007: fig. 4.22, nos 5-7) and Glazed Ware represent strong ties from Mesopotamia travelling via the Gulf, as might an earlier Palmyrene inscription (Sedov 1992: 118). A sizeable presence of Aksumite pottery, bolstered by three coins (Sedov & 'Aydarus 1995: 53), reflects political relations with East Africa. Contact with India was 'reduced drastically' during this period (Sedov 2007: 105).

North-east of Qana was the capital of the Hadramawt, Shabwa (Saubatha of *PME* 27), where the royal palace was situated and where caravan and sea routes converged. An inscription indicates that two each of Palmyrenes, Indians and Chaldeans were in the area for the investiture of an early third-century king (Breton 1989: 184). External influences are visible in many aspects of material life, such as architecture (e.g. Audouin 1991: 178). Another focal point for the overland trade was the Qataban capital at Timna. Here too foreign influences are detected – most famously a pair of bronze lions ridden by boyish figures with a South Arabian inscription (Segall 1958).

Each of these inland sites boasts a range of imported pottery, not unexpectedly with a higher ratio of Roman fine or table wares to amphorae than the ports. Although in limited quantity, Shabwa has a diverse array of amphorae, fine and coarse wares from the first to fourth centuries AD from the Western Mediterranean (including ITS), Egypt, the Aegean and Syria, and Mesopotamian Glazed Ware (Badré 1991, see also Rutten 2007: 17; Calvet 1988; Breton 2003: 204, 207). Late Roman pottery is represented by a potential Aqaba amphora (Breton 2003: 209, citing Ballet & Lemaître forthcoming). Foreign coins are rare, but include one each of Ptolemaic, Late Roman and Aksumite (Sedov & 'Aydarus 1995: 53). At Timna there is an exotic range of Augustan fine wares, particularly

Italian and Syrian *sigillata*, glazed wares from Asia Minor and Egyptian faience (Comfort 1958).

Moscha Limen (Khor Rori) is said to have been refounded by colonists from Shabwa in the late first century BC/early first century AD in order to guard the frankincense region (Sedov 2007: 100, citing Robin 1984). It has been generally accepted that the main purpose of Khor Rori was to supply Qana with incense. According to the *Periplus* (*PME* 32), Indian ships sometimes spent the winter at Khor Rori rather than Qana, due to the lateness of the season. The site was excavated by Albright in the 1950s, and since 1997 Italian excavations have led Avanzini to argue that monumental architecture such as city walls, a gate and temples would not have been needed if Khor Rori was merely a satellite of Qana (Albright 1982; Avanzini 2002: 20-5). In 2001 Avanzini and Orazi suggested that the early settlement, dating to the late first century BC, was established to defend harbours and trade routes, and that in the first century AD it became a city with one of the most intricate defensive systems seen in South Arabia. A more recent chronology tentatively suggests that it was founded before Qana in the third century BC to facilitate Hadrami trade with the Gulf and Oman (Avanzani 2002: 21; Avanzini & Sedov 2005: 15). Its refounding, in the late first century BC/early first century AD, would make Khor Rori and Qana virtually contemporaneous. The end of the city is more difficult to place. Based on South Arabian coinage and a $^{14}$C date from the gate complex, Avanzini has suggested a date in the fifth or sixth century with the demise of Hadrami autonomy (Avanzini 2002: 24); however, imported pottery ceased around the late fourth/early fifth century (Sedov & Benvenuti 2002: 191).

The ceramic assemblage from Khor Rori is similar to that of the Lower and Middle periods of Qana, although in reduced quantity (ibid.: 191-5; Comfort 1960). The presence of Hadrami Organic Storage Jars, the 'Palestinian' storage jars that are probably Torpedoes, and Glazed Ware further allies the site with Qana. Importantly, the assemblage at Khor Rori does not extend into the Upper period of Qana with the attendant Late Roman amphorae. The absence of Aksumite wares is another significant distinction. Sedov and Benvenuti attribute the smaller quantity of imported storage jars/amphorae at Khor Rori to site function, and suggest that they were intended for use on the site, while at Qana they were for both use and export (ibid.: 192). Nor does Khor Rori appear to have the basalt from the Qana region that was exported to the Egyptian Red Sea ports (Peacock et al. 2007: 62), further evidence for Khor Rori as a facilitator for Qana rather than an overseas port in its own right.

Sedov (2007: 102) believes that there were foreign residents at Qana, and the quantity of Indian cooking vessels suggests some were Indians. Indian artefacts from the Lower period at Qana are numerically insignificant, but are much more common by the Middle period (ibid.: 102, 104). Sedov and Benvenuti draw attention to a class of cooking pots that form the most common cooking vessel at both Khor Rori and Qana (2002: 192-4; e.g. pl. 15). They are cautious in attributing these vessels to India, as although slipped they do not belong to RPW, instead to CRSW. The problem here lies in the definition of RPW (Schenk in press). These cooking pots can be sourced to India although, unlike RPW, need not come from the North. Other Indian wares include storage jars (Sedov & Benvenuti 2002: pl. 3, nos 2-3) and Organic Black Ware (ibid.: pl. 16, nos 2-4). At Khor Rori, Indian pottery is matched by rare Indian finds of a bronze statue of a female (Albright 1955) and a coin of Kanishka (Sedov & 'Aydarus 1995: 53).

*PME* 57 notes that Qana was an embarkation point for ships to North and South India:

... some leave directly from Kane and some from the

Promontory of Spices, and whoever are bound for Limyrike hold out with the wind on the quarter for most of the way, but whoever are bound for Barygaza and whoever for Skythia only three days and no more ...

The role of South Arabia in reference to the journey to India, and its relation with the Red Sea, will be explored in Chapter 6.

### Crossroads of the ocean (Figs 15 and 17)

The Indian Ocean island of Socotra or Dioscurides is strategically located. The closest landmass is Cape Guardafui, but during the time of the *Periplus* it was subject to South Arabia. *PME* 30-1 describes it as an inhospitable place and downplays its resources, and Casson (1989: 170; Singer 2007: 22) suggests that exports travelled via South Arabia, although equally 'Arabs, Indians and even some Greeks' live on the north side of the island (*PME* 30). Historically Socotra was famed for 'Dragon's blood' or Indian cinnabar (red resin) and aloe. Its importance as a meeting point between East and West is demonstrated by text fragments that tell of Abyssinian (East African), West Indian, South Arabian, Armenian and Palmyrene visitors during the Early Roman period (De Geest 2006: 19). References to Abyssinians contradict the notion that Socotra was excluded from the Egypt-Africa route (Casson 1989: 167). Ships on their way to India from the Red Sea may have coasted along the African shore to the Promontory of Spices and stopped off at Socotra (Hourani 1995: 29).

Archaeologically, Socotra is mostly known through surface survey. Finds that can be assigned to the period of Indo-Roman trade have been identified on the north-east at Hajrya, where some excavation has been conducted (Naumkin & Sedov 1995: 224-9; Sedov 2007: 100). Investigated by a Russian-Yemeni team in 1985 and 1987, it was a defended settlement with a cemetery within massive walls. Although extending into the Islamic period, earlier wares included a Roman amphora handle, sherds from the Gulf and handmade jars of the first to fourth centuries AD, similar to some from Wadi Hadramawt and Qana (Naumkin & Sedov 1995: 229, fig. 19, no. 1, fig. 20, no. 8).

### *Terra incognita*: the Persian/Arabian Gulf (Fig. 18)

Of all the regions involved in Indo-Roman trade, the Gulf was the most separate, both geographically and politically. Mesopotamian ceramics – both Torpedo jars and Glazed Ware – dominate the assemblages. It appears that the writer of the *Periplus* had first-hand knowledge only to around Khor Rori; thereafter, continuing through the Straits of Hormuz, and into the Gulf, information was limited (*PME* 33-7). Salles has suggested that this lack of clarity is because the Gulf was controlled by Arab-Persian merchants (1993: 513). Two ports are mentioned: Apologos, at the head of the Gulf (*PME* 35) near modern Basra; the second, Omana (*PME* 36-7), on the Arabian side, is more difficult to place and although much debated Ed Dur has been considered the most likely candidate (Potts 1990: 309; Haerinck 1998a: 275). However, sizeable quantities of first-century AD imports, especially Mesopotamian Glazed Ware, Roman glass and jewellery and etched carnelian beads from India, recently excavated from a tomb at Dibba al-Hisn, have revived the debate, so that Dibba has been proposed as an alternative site for Omana (Jasim 2006).

Ed Dur and its more inland neighbour, Mleiha, are the two most extensively excavated sites on the Arabian side of the Gulf. Ed Dur, on the Oman Peninsula, is positioned so that it cannot be seen from the sea. The site was extensively excavated by Belgian, French, English and Danish teams between 1986 and 1995. Its origins lie in the Iron Age but it was then abandoned until its main occupation which spanned the

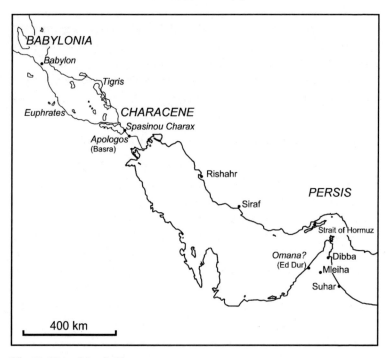

Fig. 18. Map of the Gulf.

second half of the first century BC to the early second century AD, when it covered *c*. 2-3 km$^2$. After a hiatus a second revival, primarily of a religious/funerary nature, occurred during the third/fourth centuries on a smaller, intermittent scale (Lecomte 1993; Haerinck 1998b: 24). The most substantial structural remains include rock-cut graves or shaft entrance tombs, some rock-carved beach-front buildings and a temple; many of the domestic buildings were probably constructed of more ephemeral materials, such as palm branches (Salles 1993: 501-2). Most structures belong to the first century AD; the largest building seems to have served as a funerary temple and is associated with the ritual slaughter of a camel *c*. AD 225-300 (Potts 1990: 276-9).

110

## 4. Beyond the Roman world

The imported finds at Ed Dur reflect a variety of sources. The coins from the early occupation phase number 32 with Characene, Hadramawt, Persis/Parthian, Nabataean, Roman and Indian ones represented (Haerinck 1998a: 297). Most of these source areas are mirrored by other categories of finds, including jewellery, metal and ceramics. Worth noting are beads from India, Sri Lanka and Tanzania (ibid.: 296-7).

Glass is perhaps the most spectacular imported find with a number of substantial or complete vessels. The 227 vessels from the Belgian and Danish excavations reported on by Whitehouse form a cohesive group dated to the period between *c.* 25 BC and AD 75; the majority are Roman with a small number of Parthian vessels (1998, 2000). Twenty of the 122 vessels from the Belgian excavation came from a collective tomb (Whitehouse 1998: 64). Funerary glass occurred alongside other luxury items; for example, one tomb contained a Roman glass beaker, a range of small items and an elaborate bronze wine set in a pre-Hellenistic tradition of a type also known from Mleiha (Potts 1989: 15; Mouton 1992: 109-11).

In contrast to the glass, Roman pottery is rare with Mesopotamian Glazed Ware and Torpedo jars much more common (Mouton 1992). Roman types include two amphora sherds, one a body sherd from an indeterminate Western source with a Latin stamp of 'LNV' (Papadopoulos 1994). Rutten's (2007) summary of the Roman fine wares from Ed Dur identifies 36 sherds: 29 Eastern and Western *sigillata* (including ESA, ESB, ITS), Roman glazed wares from Asia Minor and Egyptian lamps. The lack of Indian pottery is notable, as is the general lack of imported finds from the third/fourth centuries AD.

The diversity of imports suggests that Ed Dur was prosperous especially during the first century AD, but whether foreigners were present, or it was a transhipment centre, or both, is not known. The small numbers of Roman fine ware are

111

primarily from domestic contexts and thought to result from trade rather than being selected by and for Roman residents (ibid.: 20).

Mleiha is *c.* 50 km from the coast and 70 km from Ed Dur. Its origins are earlier than those of Ed Dur, with the most intense occupation taking place during the third century and first half of the second century BC, afterwards contracting. There was a slight expansion, probably in the late second or third century AD, not in size but in the construction of a fort that served as a residence, perhaps for a political ruler who oversaw food storage and craft specialists (Benoist et al. 2003: 72). In the fourth century it was abandoned. As at Ed Dur there was extensive funerary activity, but at Mleiha mudbrick houses were also common. Not mentioned in the *Periplus*, it may be Ptolemy's Ravana (*Geography* 6.7), a seat of royal residence (Groom 1994: 203) with Ed Dur in its territory (Haerinck 1998b: 27-8).

Here too foreign coins (17) are found, most from the second half of the first century BC and the first century AD. Sources are nearly identical to those of coins from Ed Dur, although there are fewer of each type apart from Arabian and an additional, single Seleucid coin. With two such small samples, it is unwise to attach too much significance to these differences, but their function warrants consideration. Haerinck suggests that foreign trade was more commonly barter, for items such as the renowned pearls of the region, rather than monetary transactions (1998b: 29-30). The relative importance of coins from Characene at both sites indicates its far-reaching influence in regional exchange (ibid.: 32). By the third century Sasanian coins were present in the region, but not at either Mleiha or Ed Dur (Haerinck 1998a: 299, citing Potts & Cribb 1995).

Other imported finds from Mleiha are similar to those from Ed Dur, such as glass from funerary contexts (Jasim 1999) and

4. Beyond the Roman world

Mesopotamian Glazed Ware and Torpedoes. Classical pottery is even rarer. Amphorae pertain to an earlier Hellenistic phase, as may a sherd of ESA illustrated by Mouton (1992: 106, fig. 86.5). During its final phases foreign imports have been identified alongside more regional ones, the latter including probable Indian pottery (Benoist et al. 2003: 66-71, n. 16, fig. 9.4-6). Also present is an Egyptian amphora (ibid.: fig. 9.1) which the excavators rely upon to date their sequence to the late second/third century, but it could be from earlier in the second century. Although in absolute quantity Ed Dur has many more imported finds than Mleiha, Mouton attributes this to intensive excavation and the type of features explored at Ed Dur (1999: 25).

What then was the relationship between the two sites? One theory is that Ed Dur was the port for Mleiha and the two had a symbiotic relationship: Ed Dur supplied Mleiha with seafoods and foreign objects, while Mleiha was rich in agricultural products; furthermore, they shared a local coinage restricted to the Oman Peninsula (Haerinck 1998b: esp. 27). Mouton, however, has challenged this interpretation, arguing that there is little evidence for seaborne trade at Ed Dur. Instead he suggests that the imported finds at both sites could result from the Arabian caravan route until the final period at Mleiha, when Indian and Egyptian pottery was related to activity at the later site of Suhar, not Ed Dur (Mouton 1999: 24-5; Benoist et al. 2003: 72).

On the Iranian side of the Gulf fewer sites have been excavated and most are known only through survey, particularly that conducted by Andrew Williamson between 1968 and 1971 (Priestman 2005: fig. 3). Williamson's pottery has recently been assessed and a range of Indian types including RPW identified (ibid.: fig. 29). Earlier, Whitehouse and Williamson mapped RPW in the region and concluded that 'without doubt [they] were imported as a by-product of maritime trade between the Gulf ports and Scythia ...' (1973: 39, fig. 7).

Williamson identified a port at Rishahr in the Bushire Peninsula with a potentially pre-Islamic fort. Surface finds suggest that the site was occupied in the Partho-Sasanian period; it may have been attacked from the Arabian coast, during the reign of Shapur II (AD 383-88), but by the fifth century was re-established as a seat of Nestorian Christianity (ibid.: 35-42). Whitehouse and Williamson advanced the theory that after Rishahr was plundered, Shapur shifted his base to Siraf – the only excavated site on the Persian side of the Gulf (ibid.: 42). Despite a fort with similarities to Roman installations in Iraq (ibid.: 33), the recovery of more than 30 Sasanian coins across the site (11 datable ones between the fourth/fifth and early seventh centuries) and two Roman coins (one each of Theodosius I and Constans II) (Lowick 1985: 1-2, 11-15), there is no stratigraphic evidence for pre-Islamic levels at Siraf. The importance of the site as an international port instead dates from *c.* AD 800 (Whitehouse & Williamson 1973: 42). The Roman coins are part of a sprinkling of Late Roman ones identified from Mesopotamia and the Gulf, whose function is not obvious (Hobbs 1995).

A number of key sites in the Gulf demonstrate a combination of Mesopotamian, Roman and Indian finds. Late deposits are rare and lack substantial Roman assemblages on the scale of Qana. Although quantity cannot always be evaluated, Mesopotamian pottery is the most common, Roman and Indian are sparse, with Indian increasing during the Early Islamic period. Glass and other finds quantitatively boost the Roman component. The sparse Roman finds are in keeping with the lack of information in the *Periplus*; interpreted as reflecting the enmity between Parthians and Romans that continued into the Sasanian period (Bharucha-Irani 2002: 71-2; contra Salles 1993: 498).

114

## 4. Beyond the Roman world

Returning to the *Periplus*, *PME* 36 describes Omana as a place where ships from Barygaza both import and export, which would account for Indian finds at either Dibba or Ed Dur. Salles has suggested that Roman items may have reached the Gulf as re-exported items from Barygaza, although Barygaza cannot be evaluated archaeologically (1993: 516-17). Schoff put forward a similar hypothesis for the re-export of Western copper from India to the Gulf (1912: 151). Certainly the *Periplus* describes the export of wood and copper from India to Apologos and Omana (*PME* 36; Casson 1989: 28-9), but there is no evidence that this is Western copper rather than Indian. An early fifth-century Babylonian Talmudic writing refers to the importation of *Hinduan* [Indian] iron into Mesopotamia (Lang et al.1988: 11), indicating that at this later date at least some of the metal travelling through the Gulf was Indian. If Roman material was filtered to the Gulf via non-Roman ports then Qana, which received Western copper (*PME* 28) and archaeologically has a wealth of Roman finds, was a more likely transhipment point than an Indian port.

Another possibility is that Roman material travelled overland from Palmyra to the head of the Gulf at Apologos, where it was exported to the Gulf. This and another overland route through Babylonia and Charax have proponents in Whitehouse (2000: 121-2) and Haerinck (1998b: 31, 1998a: 284, 292). It provides an explanation for the large quantities of Mesopotamian Glazed Ware in the Gulf, particularly if the Basra area is one source (Kennet 2004: 30), and a likely point for its export (Lang et al. 1988: 11). It would also provide an explanation for the Roman glass ware in the Gulf, as yet missing from Qana. Early Islamic writers refer to Basra as the 'Gateway to India' (ibid.: 11, citing Friedman 1992: 15-16) and Indians were resident as a minority population within the Sasanian state (ibid., citing Morony 1984: 271-2).

In her excellent synthesis of *sigillata* in the Gulf and Indian

115

Ocean, Rutten has closely examined trade routes, incorporating the evidence from Mesopotamia (2007: 17-19). She argues forcibly that some of the ESA reached Ed Dur via Mesopotamia during the late first century BC/AD, but that a second more important route distributed Roman fine wares to the Gulf through a Red Sea-South Arabian link, re-exported from Qana and Khor Rori. This Qana/Omana route (*PME* 36) was used for distributing frankincense, some of which has been collected at Ed Dur alongside the other South Arabia imports described above (ibid.: 19).

# 5

# Lands to the East

### India and its north-south divide (Figs 19 and 21)

As a region, India presents the greatest challenge because of its diversity. In *The Personality of India*, Subbarao outlined the importance of India's geography (1956: 4-7). He argued that the large alluvial plains of the Indus and Ganges, the physical barriers formed by numerous mountains and river systems and the coastline with anchorages are instrumental in its cultural and historical development. These geographical features have facilitated both overland and sea migration of foreigners and at the same time ensured their assimilation. Subbarao furthermore characterised three different zones by their accessibility and interaction, as areas of attraction, relative isolation and isolation (ibid.; see also Morrison 2002: n. 1). On the basis of these same geographical features, Subbarao and others conventionally divide India into three main regions: the Himalayan uplands, the Indo-Gangetic plains and peninsular India (1956: 7; Thapar 2002: 39). Each is further divided into complex sub-zones that can be compared to the *tinai* (eco-zones) defined in the *Sangam* poetry for South India (Gurukkal 1995). Overall, the importance of the coastline cannot be overstressed, particularly when studying long-distance economy and trade, for not only did it provide numerous entry points for maritime contacts, but it also created foci for kingdoms with maritime links (Thapar 2002: 46).

Geographically and politically the north and south are distinct. Peninsular India – the Deccan Plateau and the four

117

Dravidian states of Karnataka, Andhra Pradesh, Tamil Nadu and Kerala – has the greatest mineral wealth (Ray 1996: 351). Ray describes the most agriculturally fertile areas of peninsular India as the deltas that connect via the coast, while the links between the peninsula and the north are mainly overland (ibid.). In the following sections, the South is defined as Tamil Nadu and Kerala or 'Tamilakam', which was organised by chiefdoms, as opposed to the monarchies found further to the north.

Chronologically the period of Roman contact is subsumed mostly within the Indian Early Historic period. Parameters for the Early Historic period vary as a result of different cultural developments throughout the continent, the degree of urbanism and how it can be measured. In the Ganges Valley, for example, the beginning of the period could be placed as early as the sixth century BC. Generally, however, a date of 300

**Key to Fig. 19**

| | | |
|---|---|---|
| 1. Adam | 23. Karaikadu | 46. Paithan |
| 2. Ajabpura | 24. Karnaji | 47. Palghat |
| 3. Akota | 25. Karur | 48. *Patala* |
| 4. Alagankulam | 26. Karvana | 49. Pattanam |
| 5. Anuradhapura | 27. Kateshwar | 50. Paunar |
| 6. Arikamedu | 28. Kaveripattinam | 51. Prabhas-Somnath |
| 7. *Bakare* | 29. Kolhapur | 52. Rajbadidanga |
| 8. *Barbarikon* | 30. *Komar* | 53. Sanand |
| 9. Begram | 31. Kondapur | 54. Sanjan |
| 10. Bet Dwarka | 32. Korkai | 55. Shamalaji |
| 11. Bharuch | 33. Lothal | 56. *Sopatma* |
| 12. Chandraketugarh | 34. Madurai | 57. Tamluk |
| 13. Chaul | 35. Maligamedu | 58. Taxila |
| 14. Coimbatore | 36. Mangalore | 59. Ter |
| 15. Devnimori | 37. Manikpatna | 60. Tilda |
| 16. Dwarka | 38. Mantai | 61. Tirukkoilur |
| 17. Elephanta | 39. Mathura | 62. Tissamaharama |
| 18. Hathab | 40. Mylapore | 63. *Tyndis* |
| 19. Iyyal | 41. Nagara | 64. Ujjain |
| 20. Junnar | 42. Nani Rayan | 65. Vallabipur |
| 21. Kamrej | 43. Nasik | 66. Vasavasamudram |
| 22. Kanchipuram | 44. *Nelkynda* | 67. Vellalore |
| | 45. Nevasa | |

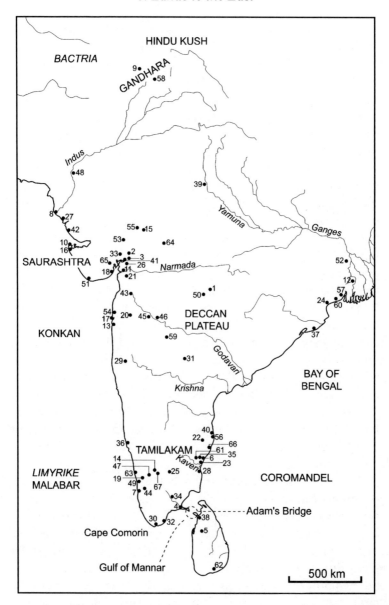

Fig. 19. Map of India and Sri Lanka.

119

BC is applied. In both North and South India, the Early Historic period was marked by the widespread occurrence of Ashokan inscriptions in the third century BC (Chakrabarti 1999: 262-4) when most of India belonged to the Mauryan Empire (*c.* 325-184 BC). Once the Early Historic period was established there were important similarities in material culture throughout India, including bricks and tiles, pottery types and more extensive use of coinage (ibid.: 315-18).

In the north the Early Historic period is normally terminated between AD 300 and 500, coinciding loosely with the beginning and end of the Gupta era. Conventionally, in the south a terminal date of AD 300 has been adopted, but this is largely based on what has been considered the end of the Roman contact period. Whether Roman contact ended then or, more importantly, whether this is an appropriate measure to define the Early Historic period, must be considered. Already Roman finds of the sixth or even early seventh century have been identified and therefore spill over into what is considered the Early Medieval period. In both north and south the definition is fluid and requires ongoing review. Certainly within this broad timeframe, changes in the organisation of trade took place (Chakravarti 2002: 26). Already Selvakumar and Darsana (2008) have proposed a chronology for the southern Early Historic period that culminates at AD 500, and Ray has drawn attention to numerous third-/fourth-century sites on the Andhra Pradesh coast (1996: 358).

As noted above, North India belonged to an established tradition of urbanism that was in place long before the arrival of Alexander in the north-west in 327-325 BC. This is evidenced by the presence of such features as a settlement hierarchy that included large centres, craft specialisation, external trade links and coinage. More than any other region of India, it was the entry point for successive waves of foreign invasions or migrations, not only Greek, but others from Central Asia and

Persia. In the East Deccan and South India the Early Historic period marked the transition from a megalithic to a more urbanised society as a result of inter-regional trade (Champakalakshmi 2006: 92).

The stimulus of maritime commerce with the West and Southeast Asia may have played a part in this transition, but views are widely divergent. Some scholars, such as Champakalakshmi (ibid.) see it as essential to growth, Ray and others view it as one of many stimuli (1995b; Thapar 1997: 21, 30), and Gurukkal as not affecting economic and social development (1995: 250). Generalisations about India are difficult because of regional differences, but exchange and trade is one feature that forms a connecting thread through this diversity (Thapar 2002: 234, 245).

Intertwined with trade is another connecting thread – that of Buddhism. Although Buddhism was not causal, from Mauryan times its ideology fostered trade growth on both internal and maritime routes (Ray 1998: 8, 122-43, 189; Chakravarti 2002: 24, 31). The effect of Buddhism differed between regions and was least visible in the south. In Bengal and Orissa it was a significant force, and was particularly marked in the Deccan. In the western Deccan market centres followed major routes and were associated with Buddhist monastic settlements, while in the eastern Deccan Buddhist centres were related to existing Megalithic sites (Ray 1995b, 1998: 30-3, 191-2).

Five regions are described below that reflect political and cultural developments in the post-Mauryan age, although their boundaries and alliances varied through time. The sites discussed are guided by those with Western or purportedly Western finds. Only a minority of the inhabited settlements of this period have imports, which in turn comprise only a small proportion of their assemblages. Most of the economy was based on local and regional trade networks, and even large centres did not necessarily participate in long-distance trade (Smith 2002), or at least this is not materially visible.

Many, but certainly not all, sites with imported finds are located on the coast. Given the ferocity of the waters surrounding India many ports are some distance from the coast, sited on river estuaries that served to facilitate inland trade. Ray attributes their prosperity not to their coastal location but to the wealth of their hinterland (1995a: 98). Siltation means that many sites are now further away from waterways than in Antiquity.


## The north-west: Taxila and Begram

This consists of the area between the Indus and the north of the Hindu Kush. Its importance lies in overland rather than coastal routes, but we will nevertheless touch on it because of two key sites in the region. Taxila, now in Pakistan, is famous as the place where Alexander the Great sojourned after he crossed the Indus; subsequently he reached the head of the Indus delta at Patala before travelling West in retreat. The importance of Taxila lies in its strategic location, on trade routes from Bactria and Central Asia, but also with access to the Indus system leading to the Arabian Sea (Chakrabarti 2004: 285). Here Iranian, Indian and, eventually, Hellenistic elements merged (Thapar 2002: 157).

Large-scale excavations at Taxila were carried out primarily by Sir John Marshall between 1913 and 1945, although Wheeler excavated there in 1944-5 (Chakrabarti 2004: 285-91). Taxila comprises three main sites. One of them, Sirkap, is most relevant to our interests with mostly Saka-Pahlava (Scytho-Parthian) period remains that indicate an affluent population and the material influences that these names denote. Roman finds date to the first century AD, including metal, glass, gems (Whitehouse 1989: 95), a Dressel 2-4 amphora (Marshall 1975: 408, fig. 121, no. 15) and a coin of Tiberius (Turner 1989: 78). Located at the convergence of trade routes, Whitehouse believes that, via Barbarikon, Taxila received Roman objects and exported goods from central and eastern Asia (1989: 95).

Taxila is equally important as the capital of Gandhara, which during the Kushana period (second century BC to AD 230) produced a unique style in art, merging Buddhist themes and Classical styles. Whether Hellenistic or Roman influence was more significant is unresolved (Ball 2001: 139-48; Whitehouse 1989). Gandharan art has an effect throughout the continent, since its Classical affinities are in part responsible for the exaggeration of Roman finds in India. Many objects previously thought to be Roman are now considered Indian, some because of the influence of Gandhara such as architectural fragments decorated with acanthus from Devnimori (Mehta & Chowdhory 1966: 124-5, fig. 47). Others represent the copying of Classical themes or techniques by local craftsmen. Examples in Fig. 20 include a bronze statue of a Classical figure from Shamalaji normally described as Atlas (Chowdhary 1962: fig. 1), and an intaglio of an Indian woman tooled on a pottery sherd from Arikamedu that has been invoked as evidence for a Western inspired local gem-carving industry (Begley 1996: 29, fig. 1.13).

The second site is Begram, now in Afghanistan. Also Kushana, it formed a crossroads for caravan routes between the Mediterranean and India, and from the Wakhan corridor of Afghanistan to China (Whitehouse 1989: 95). A spectacular cache, from what is interpreted as a royal palace, includes bronze, rock crystal, glass and plaster models for metalworkers from the Mediterranean in association with Indian and Chinese objects. Microprobe analysis on a very small number of samples indicates an Egyptian source for some of the glass. Conventionally the deposit was thought to have gradually

Fig. 20. Indian objects that show Roman influence.
Left: Bronze Classical figure from Shamalaji (after Chowdhary 1962: figs 1-3).
Right: Indian-figure intaglio on a ceramic sherd from Arikamedu (after Begley 1996: fig. 1.13).

accumulated from the first century BC to its deposition in the third century. However, Whitehouse has reassessed the dating, primarily for the 150+ objects of glass, and concluded that they were probably deposited within a generation of AD 100 (ibid.: 99).

## Gujarat and the Konkan Coast:
## Barbarikon and Barygaza

This region includes the main area of the Western Khastrapas (AD 35-405) in the modern states of Gujarat and the coastal area of Maharashtra, incorporating foci of the western coast such as the Indus Delta, Saurashtra and the Konkan (Thapar 2002: 46). There are two main river systems here: the Indus, connecting the area to eastern India as well as to the Arabian Sea and ultimately the West; and the Narmada, flowing into central India. Like the north-west it has a long tradition of external contacts and shared not only a border but cultural affinities with the Kushana Empire to its north and north-west. It, too, was subject to successive foreign influences from the Indo-Greeks, Indo-Scythians, Indo-Parthians, Kushanas and Sasanians.

The Greco-Roman sources name two important sites in this region, neither of which is well known archaeologically. The most northerly is Barbarikon (*PME* 39), a port strategically located on the mouth of the Indus in modern Pakistan that served the royal capital at Minnagar, at an unspecified spot further up the river.

The second, Barygaza (Bharuch), is mentioned more than any other single place in the *Periplus* – 28 times in 19 of the 66 chapters (Casson 1989: 200, 277), despite its treacherous approach described in *PME* 43-6. Barygaza was located on the northern bank of the Narmada River, *c.* 30 km from the mouth where the first safe anchorage lies (Howell & Sinha 1994: 197). Its importance reflects the richness of Barygaza's hinterland, connecting the port with three different routes: to Bactria, the Ganges Valley and the lower Krishna Valley (Ray 1998: 27). Barygaza was not only a port, but a manufacturing centre (Casson 1989: 22); like Barbarikon it was a transhipment point for goods from the East, in this case via Ozene (Ujjain) (*PME* 48). Mehta (1957) conducted a survey in the region in the 1950s and each subsequent decade has seen further work there, all hindered by medieval and modern occupation. A range of Early Historic finds has been recorded, including typical pottery from the south bank opposite Bharuch and at sites *c.* 10-15 km downriver (Howell & Sinha 1994: 198). Shinde et al. describe 'A thick well-fired fragment of a jar, possibly a Mediterranean amphora ...' (2002: 74). A sherd of LR1 in the M.S. Baroda University storeroom came from a tin labelled 'Broach' (Bharuch) that contained finds from a number of Mehta's finds, so the site attribution to Bharuch is only tentative. The

*Periplus* mentions that in the region of Barygaza there 'are still preserved to this very day signs of Alexander's expedition, ancient shrines and the foundations of encampments and huge wells' (*PME* 41), but Thapar concludes that Alexander left little impact on India, historically or politically (2002: 157).

Although the finds from these important sites are disappointing in terms of long-distance interests, relevant material has been identified elsewhere in the region, including Early and Late Roman and particularly Mesopotamian amphorae shown in Fig. 21. This variety of imported amphorae reflects the long-term trade interests of the region and successive foreign influences. The identification of Torpedo jars as the most common of the three types overturns established patterns and underlines the importance of trade via the Gulf and Parthian/Sasanian influence in the region. The small number of Roman coins recorded here (Fig. 2), where indigenous silver coinage existed, might intuitively suggest that Roman coinage entered the region to circulate within a monetary economy. However, Casson interprets the *Periplus* to mean that coinage was used for barter at Barygaza and sometimes as cash at Barbarikon (1989: 30-1; Ray 1991: 60; see Chapter 2, p. 35). The logic must be sought in the scarcity of local coins of precious metal, so that Roman ones were welcome as bullion (Turner & Cribb 1996: 312).

**Key to Fig. 21**

| | | |
|---|---|---|
| 2. Ajabpura | 21. Kamrej | 43. Nasik |
| 3. Akota | 23. Karaikadu | 45. Nevasa |
| 4. Alagankulam | 25. Karur | 46. Paithan |
| 5. Anuradhapura | 27. Kateshwar | 49. Pattanam 50. |
| 6. Arikamedu | 29. Kolhapur | Paunar |
| 10. Bet Dwarka | 33. Lothal | 51. Prabhas-Somnath |
| 13. Chaul | 35. Maligamedu | 53. Sanand |
| 15. Devnimori | 38. Mantai | 54. Sanjan |
| 16. Dwarka | 39. Mathura | 58. Taxila |
| 17. Elephanta | 40. Mylapore | 62. Tissamaharama |
| 18. Hathab | 41. Nagara | 65. Vallabipur |
| 20. Junnar | 42. Nani Rayan | 66. Vasavasamudram |

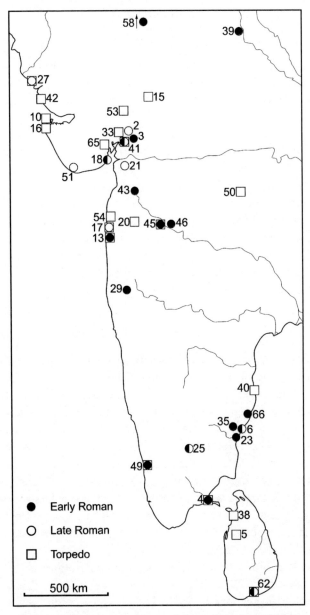

Fig. 21. Distribution map of known imported amphorae in India
and Sri Lanka. For references and sources see Endnote 2.

127

Less functional imported Roman objects are not common, but from the Early Roman period include a Roman quartz cameo from Karvana and a bronze jug handle with a relief figure of Eros straddling an amphora from Akota (Desai 1951; De Puma 1992: 101-2).

The largest concentration of amphorae in the region comes from Elephanta. Located *c.* 10 miles from Mumbai harbour, the site is best known for its caves with monumental sculptures dedicated to Shiva. Its main importance as a port was during the sixth century, the period to which the carvings date, and its wealth derived from its strategic location (Tripathi 2004: 122). Four Late Roman amphora types and Mesopotamian Torpedo jars occur, some in quantity (Table 3, p. 166). How the combination of these types reached Elephanta is of interest as no single entrepot for India contains all of them.

### The north-east: Tamluk and Chandraketugarh

This region comprises the modern states of West Bengal and Orissa. Its outstanding geographical feature is the Ganges, which feeds into the Bay of Bengal, thus positioning the region both on the Ganges Valley river systems and the coast (Ray 2006: 73). Culturally it was somewhat separate, for although part of the Mauryan Empire it thereafter became essentially autonomous until the Gupta period. Bengal may well have been ruled by immigrants originally from Central Asia (Jahan 2005), while Orissa was part of Kalinga. Thapar has suggested that in the north-east, in contrast to the north-west, the Himalayas formed a barrier, which may account in part for its cultural history (Thapar 2002: 41).

Turner's map shows a near absence of Roman coins from these states (1989: 119), but reports of Roman finds have sustained its perceived role in Indo-Roman trade (Das Gupta 1960). Many, though – including terracotta figurines – are more likely Roman inspired than Roman. Three inscriptions may be genuine imported finds, although they are no longer available for inspection (S. Jahan, D. Chakrabarti, pers. comm.). These include two Latin seals from Rajbadidanga with personal names, 'Oaborra' and 'Horae' (*IAR* 1968-9: 43), and a clay tablet from Tilda with a Greek inscription (*IAR* 1955-6: 62). Greek, however, need not signal an import since it was used by Indians, particularly in the north-west where there are several Ashokan inscriptions in Greek and Aramaic (Thapar 2002: 179-83), as well as on imitated Greek coins in western India (Cribb 2005: 9).

Roman amphorae have been reported on from Manikpatna (Gupta 1997: 353), Karnaji (Sengupta 1998: pl. 1) and Tamluk (Jahan 2006: 71). On examination, all are instead post-Roman in date: those from Tamluk and Manikpatna are salt-glazed vessels, while the Karnaji one is an Islamic earthenware jar. Jahan has also demonstrated that so-called amphorae from Chandraketugarh are local (ibid.: 72, fig. 2.7). As the most important Early Historic port in East India (Chakrabarti 2004: 302), Tamluk is the site more than any other in this region where one would expect genuine Roman artefacts. Egyptian pots were noted by Vogel in 1952 (Casson 1989: 236), but since they were not illustrated cannot be substantiated. Tamluk has been equated with Gange of the *Periplus* (*PME* 63), as a transhipment point for Gangetic nard, cotton and other items. Ptolemy (*Geography* 7.1.81) also mentioned Gange, as a royal seat; markedly he listed more sites in this region than the writer of the *Periplus*, either through greater familiarity or an increase in activity in the intervening hundred years.

Despite this lack of Roman coinage and other artefacts, regional products were fundamental items of exchange. As noted, Gangetic cotton is mentioned by the *Periplus* (*PME* 63) and could be the source of some Indian cotton in Egypt. The Muziris papyrus describes a mechanism for the exportation of

Gangetic nard, stating that some travelled via Muziris (Rathbone 2001; Casson 1986). If correct, Gogte's (1997) recent proposal that the Tamluk-Chandraketugarh area is the epicentre of RW production provides a more visible way to track exports.

In this region Indo-Roman trade is considered indirect through internal trade routes, particularly with the Coromandel Coast (Tripathi 2002: 124; Jahan 2002: 131; Ray 1996: 355). Contact between the north-east and south-east is evidenced by Indo-Pacific beads, possibly produced in Bengal by Tamil craftsmen (Jahan 2002: 132), and also the concentration of RW in the south-east. More important for the region was trade with Southeast Asia and Sri Lanka, some of which was funnelled through South India (Jahan 2002: 135; Tripathi 2002: 121). Documents indicate that only from the fourth/fifth centuries AD was travel between the Ganges delta and Sri Lanka direct by sea (Ray 1998: 23).

There is no evidence that Romans visited or lived in Bengal, but Chinese pilgrims, including Fa-hein in the early fifth century, stayed at Tamluk (Ramachandra 1951: 226-7) and Indians sent embassies from Tamluk to China in the third century (Jahan 2005: 79, 81, citing Petech 1950).

According to Jahan, trade peaked during the first century BC/AD, dropped dramatically after the second century and declined from the Gupta period onwards (Jahan 2002: 135). There is no evidence that this cycle was linked to Roman fortunes, but instead to coastal contacts throughout peninsular India and Sri Lanka (Ray 1998: 30-1).

### The Deccan: Nevasa, Kolhapur and Ter

This region includes the area between the Krishna and Godavari Rivers, and encompassed the Satavahana Empire (200 BC to AD 250) with its capital at Paithan. The Satavahanas probably originated in the west of the region and spread to the east (Thapar 2002: 226; Ray 1996: 356). In modern terms it comprises much of Maharashtra and Andhra Pradesh, skirting the top of Karnataka, although in Antiquity conflicts with their Saka neighbours meant some changes to this border through time. It was part of a flourishing network of internal trade routes that reached the coast, particularly the Konkan, for maritime trade (Chakrabarti 1999: 290). Ray has demonstrated that the origins of trade in this region were in the Mauryan period; one suggestion is that it was further developed because its strategic position and low agricultural productivity forced the development of other sources of income and interregional trade to support urban populations (1985: 15-19). By the second century this region linked North and South India politically, as well as for trade and the spread of Buddhism (Thapar 2002: 227). Satavahana influence gradually expanded into Andhra Pradesh and Karnataka in the second or third century (Ray 1995b, 1998: 191-2), and by the third and fourth centuries had broken up into a number of smaller kingdoms (Thapar 2002: 227-8).

The Krishna River in Andhra Pradesh is the second densest area for coin hoards after Coimbatore, although here they tend to be second century in date (Turner 1989: 5-6, maps 1 and 3). To Gupta this represented a shift from South India to the eastern Deccan (Ray 1985: 29), but it also supports the shift from the west to east Deccan outlined above, and the shift from the west to east coast implied by Ptolemy and the *Sangam* poems.

In addition to an amphora and gold foil beads (Sankalia 1957; Sankalia & Dikshit 1952: 110), Kolhapur boasts one of the most spectacular groups of so-called Roman finds from India, comprising a collection of indigenous and imported metal sculptures disentangled by De Puma (1992). Included alongside Indian metalwork are vessels likely to have been produced in Campania before the eruption of Vesuvius in AD 79. The group,

131

however, is not chronologically homogeneous as indicated by a statuette of Poseidon that may date as early as the third century BC, and De Puma has suggested that the bronzes were collected together to be reused at a nearby foundry (ibid.: 101).

Other well-known collections and sites frequently associated with Roman finds are not borne out by detailed study. For example, the finds from Ter or Tagara of the *Periplus* (*PME* 51) are Indian in origin, apart from some gold foil beads (Dikshit 1969: 44). The numerous ceramic lamps, which were originally interpreted as Roman (*Dawn of Civilization* 1975: 28, fig. 68), if classically influenced, derive from Hellenistic rather than Roman models (D. Bailey, pers. comm.). Published finds from the inland market town of Adam are likewise Roman-inspired rather than Roman in origin, apart from a mostly Tiberian coin hoard (Nath 1995: 152; Turner 1989: 46). Brancaccio has illustrated how, in the Deccan, external influences are present both in subject matter, including Classical and Central Asian motifs, and technical expertise (in press).

In terms of imported amphorae the most prolific site is Nevasa, a major centre and manufacturing site located at the junction of trade routes leading from the interior to the coast (Gupta 1998). Sixty-three sherds were collected by the excavators (Sankalia et al. 1960: 280). Between Sunil Gupta (Gupta et al. 2001) and myself it was possible to locate and study 15 of these, all of which date to between the first and third centuries AD. Elsewhere imported amphorae occur only rarely, including at Nasik and Junnar, where cave inscriptions in Prakrit-Brahmi by *yavanas* are also recorded (Ray 1985: 28).

## Tamilakam: Arikamedu, Alagankulam and Pattanam

Politically Tamilakam comprised the three chiefdoms of Chola, Pandya and Chera, whose settlements were gradually urbanised at this time. It is difficult to establish artefacts that are both exclusive to and unify these three groups, but Tamil-Brahmi inscriptions on caves and pottery have the strongest potential (Abraham 2003: 218). Furthermore, their boundaries were not well established and probably shifted over time. Confined within modern Tamil Nadu and Kerala, very broadly speaking, Chera lay in the west, Chola in the north-east and Pandya in the south-east. In contrast to the north, trade with the West introduced this region to distant external contact (Thapar 1997: 21).

Above all the Chola site of Arikamedu has dominated our perception of Indo-Roman trade. Approximately 4 km south of Pondicherry, Arikamedu is located on the Ariyankuppam River, today a lagoon fed by the Gingee River. In ancient times it is likely that it would have been navigable at its mouth, as it was into the seventeenth and eighteenth centuries (Begley 1996: 10). Best known from Wheeler, actually the site has an active history of investigation from 1768-71 (for a review Begley 1983: 462, 1996: 1-4; Wheeler et al. 1946: 21-2). Jouveau-Dubriel (1941) first claimed it as a Roman city and equated it with Poduke, based on various surface finds and amphorae from local digging (Begley 1996: 1-3). One of the earliest finds was an intaglio reported to bear a portrait of Augustus; it was taken to Hanoi, but although oft-cited was never illustrated and is now lost. Such findings prompted various excavations between 1941 and 1944, led by Fr. L. Faucheux. He too recovered an unfinished intaglio, this one of a cupid and bird published by Wheeler, who thought it was completed locally by Greco-Roman craftsmen (Wheeler et al. 1946: 101, pl. xxxiii, nos 11-12). In fact it was Fr. Faucheux's finds that Wheeler first saw in Pondicherry Library and they, with many of Casal's and some of Wheeler's, can still be seen in Pondicherry Museum.

Wheeler's single season of excavation in 1945 set the agenda for all subsequent research. He established a contour map of the site and from this defined the Northern and Southern Sectors, excavating trenches in each (Wheeler et al. 1946: 22-32). His chronology was based on imported wares, from which he projected a sequence between the Augustan period and, on admittedly slim evidence, *c.* AD 200. He divided the occupation into three phases according to 38 sherds of Roman *sigillata*, all of which he thought was Arretine from modern Arezzo, Italy (Slane 1996: 351). These phases were defined as pre-Arretine, Arretine and post-Arretine and all contained Roman amphorae, of which he identified 116 sherds. From this Wheeler concluded that there was Mediterranean trade or involvement at Arikamedu throughout its entire history.

In the Northern Sector Wheeler excavated a brick structure *c.* 150 ft long that he identified as a warehouse, which supported his overall interpretation of a Roman Emporium. He assigned the structure to the post-Arretine phase and dated its construction to *c.* AD 50; it, and the entire sector, was out of use by the end of the century. The Southern Sector was radically different, considered primarily industrial and dominated by two courtyards with associated brick tanks and culverts for dyeing muslin. Bead making was also identified within this sector (ibid.: 95). Wheeler thought the Southern Sector was occupied from about the mid-first century AD until the projected date of *c.* AD 200.

Following Wheeler, a French team under the direction of Casal excavated for three seasons between 1947 and 1950. Casal's excavations, although not fully published, were more extensive than Wheeler's. According to Begley, his published findings suggested important revisions that went 'largely unnoticed' (1996: 4, 12-21). Casal recognised that the site was multi-period. Importantly, he identified an earlier Megalithic phase in the Southern Sector, possibly inhabited by fishermen (ibid.: 14), thereby isolating this area as the more ancient one

134

active prior to overseas trade. Begley has dated this phase to before the late second/early first century BC, but not before the mid-third century (2004a: 2, see also 1996: 12 for an earlier interpretation). Casal also excavated a number of workshops for metal, glass, gemstones, ivory and shell that reinforced the industrial nature of the Southern Sector (Begley 1996: 18, citing Casal 1949: 28). In the Northern Sector, Casal found fragments of a wall south of the warehouse that he suggested were part of a quay (Begley 1996: 20, citing Casal & Casal 1956: 9, fig. 3).

As noted, Arikamedu has been equated with Poduke of the *Periplus* (*PME* 60; Ptolemy *Geography* 7.1.14), but surprisingly, considering that until recently it has been the key arch-aeological site in terms of Roman finds, it received only one mention in this document. Furthermore, it was mentioned not as an overseas harbour but as a place for local boats from the north and west of India, making it pivotal for understanding connections between the Malabar and Coromandel Coasts.

Arikamedu has thus sustained debate due to its richness and its enigmatic position in Indo-Roman trade. Despite both Wheeler and Casal's excavations, many questions remained, and interest in the site was reinvigorated by Vimala Begley's 1983 article 'Arikamedu Reconsidered.' Subsequently Begley conducted three seasons of excavation there between 1989 and 1992 (Begley et al. 1996, 2004). Her work has made significant contributions to the current understanding of Arikamedu, initially by establishing a grid that correlated Wheeler and Casal's trenches (Begley 1996: 14; Begley & Sidebotham 1996: 41-50). In placing her trenches, Begley essentially followed the segmentation of the site into the Northern and Southern Sectors, excavating in both areas. In analysing the site she drew on the results from all three excavation campaigns, and was able to equate one of her layers with Wheeler's Arretine phase. Begley's excavations identified potential residential areas in the Northern Sector, as well as limited evidence for industrial activity (1996: 20-1), including substantial bead and bangle making (Francis 2004: 491); at the same time she challenged the function of the tanks for dyeing (Begley 1996: 17-18, 2004a: 10). Her work has highlighted the scale of reoccupation of the site in the medieval period, first noted by Wheeler and Casal. Disturbance and erosion to the site from medieval times to the present makes it difficult to judge its size, but a recent article by Ravitchandirane has demonstrated that its extent was seriously underestimated by previous scholars (2007).

Perhaps the most important outcome of Begley's work at Arikamedu is a reassessment of the source and date of the pottery, including that collected by British and French scholars. Until recently Arikamedu held a unique position as the only Indian site to have produced Roman *sigillata*, although it has now lost this status with sherds also recovered from Alagankulam and Pattanam (see below). Reassessment of this *sigillata* has demonstrated that it included vessels not only from Italy but also from the Eastern Mediterranean (ESA, ESB) and was not uniform in date but varied between *c*. 10 BC and AD 50 (Comfort 1992; Slane 1996). Thus the warehouse need not have belonged to the post-Arretine phase but may be slightly earlier, say between the second quarter and mid-first century AD (Begley 2004a: 6-7).

Study of the amphorae has been equally rewarding. In 1992 and more fully in 1996, Will published the available amphorae from the French and British excavations. She dated most of these sherds, and subsequently the assemblage from Begley's excavation, between the second century BC and the later first century AD (1996: 320, 2004: 328-9). The second century BC date was derived from the Greek Koan amphorae, which Will calculated as representing over 40% and 56% of the assemblages (Will 2004: 326-9). Slane, however, has presented an argument preferred here, dating the Koan amphorae to the first century BC and Augustan period, with other amphorae continuing into the second century AD (1992: 204-5). On the basis of two Knidian stamps, Tchernia suggested a start date of the early first century BC (1997b: 261). Although the peak of occupation appears to be between 50 BC and 50 AD (Begley 1996: 12), there is evidence for later occupation from six Tamil-Brahmi graffiti dated to the third century (Begley 2004a: 11-12) and the handle of a LR1 that could date to the fifth century (Will 2004: 383, no. 279). Two other potentially late sherds (Will 1996: nos 78 and 80) are discounted here.

There may be patterning in the distribution, with the majority of Greek amphorae found in the Northern Sector (Begley 2004c: 114). In addition to the wide source areas for Eastern (Kos, Knidos, Rhodes, Turkey) and Western (Italy, Gaul, Spain, North Africa) Mediterranean pottery published by Will, I have identified amphorae from Egypt – both Nile Valley and Mareotis products, and an Organic Storage Jar from the Hadramawt.

Other Mediterranean finds are lamps, glass vessels and beads (including gold foil). Coins are rare, represented by three *denarii* of Tiberius (one imitated) of questionable provenance (Berghaus 1991) and a copper of Constantine I bought in a local market (Begley 1996: 6). This paucity is in stark contrast with the other categories of finds and also with central Tamil Nadu and Kerala, although Krishnamurthy's recent finds of Late Roman coins from *c.* 75 km east at Tirukkoilur are an interesting new development (2007).

Classically inspired carved gems, such as the cupid mentioned above, are now considered to be worked by local craftsmen with Greco-Roman influence (pp. 123, 133 and Fig. 20; Begley 1996: 29-30; Sidebotham 1996a). Quantitatively these intaglios are dwarfed by the thriving glass and stone bead industries (Francis 2004). Some local pottery, too, was influenced by Hellenistic and Roman craftsmen or prototypes, as can be seen in a number of the vessel shapes (Wheeler et al. 1946: 40-1; Slane 1992: 209-10; Begley 1992: 157-76).

Other Coromandel sites mentioned in *PME* 60 alongside Poduke are Kamara and Sopatma. Kamara equates to Ptolemy's Chaberis (*Geography* 7.1.13; Casson 1989: 228) in turn identified on the ground at Kaveripattinam, a major Chola port situated on the mouth of the Kaveri River. The *Sangam Pattinappalai* depicts Kaveripattinam as a transhipment point: for items from Sri Lanka and within India from the Ganges region, Korkai and other east coast sites, and gold, gems and pepper from the interior (De Romanis 1997b: 114-16). The fifth-century *Cilappatikaram* portrays Westerners residing at Kaveripattinam around the time of Ptolemy (ibid.: 119, n. 165), although its reliability, written *c.* 300 years after Ptolemy, has been questioned (Seland 2007b: 71-2).

Terrestrial and underwater exploration around Kaveripattinam has revealed extensive Early Historic and later occupation, including a submerged, potential wharf (*IAR* 1962-3: 13). Despite reports of Roman amphorae (Rao et al. 1995-6), none have been located by this writer or by other archaeologists currently working in the region (S. Vasanthi, pers. comm.). Instead, Roman amphorae come from sites not mentioned in the *Periplus*: Vasavasamudram (Nagaswamy & Majeed 1978), Karaikadu (Raman 1992) and Alagankulam (Sridhar 2005).

It is difficult to assess the quantity of imported finds from these sites relative to Arikamedu, since they have been less extensively investigated. The most detailed archaeological information comes from Alagankulam, on the Vaigai River leading to the turbulent Gulf of Mannar. It has been correlated with the important Pandya port of Saliyur, in turn Salour of Ptolemy (*Geography* 7.1.11; Sridhar 2005: 5-6; Warmington 1928: 62). Today much of the site is heavily occupied, but where visible, surface finds are prolific with imported amphorae detected on a cursory visit. Published finds include a range of Roman pottery and six Roman coins from the late fourth and early fifth centuries (Sridhar 2005: 23, pl. 1, 83-6). This includes three *sigillata* sherds that, like those from Arikamedu, are from more than one source – in this case Italy and Asia Minor (ESB). Also, like Arikamedu, the site was occupied from the Megalithic period, with external contacts from the first century BC/AD.

If the coins are any indication, the later period at Alagankulam was substantial and may well represent a shift in importance from Arikamedu to here. Relations intensified with Sri Lanka during this period and Alagankulam was within closer reach of the island than Arikamedu, a journey estimated by Champakalakshmi as about 25 minutes by boat (2006: 133). The presence of African Red Slip Ware at Alagankulam has been extensively cited in support of a Late Roman date, but it is now accepted as Indian RW (Sridhar 2005: 26-7).

An important resource of the Gulf of Mannar was pearls, which alongside goods from the north-east and the interior were exported from the Coromandel. The Coimbatore region particularly contributed beryls (aquamarine and emerald), but other gems as well (Rajan 1998: 103; Francis 2004: 480-1). In this context the most important site would have been Karur (Ptolemy *Geography* 7.1.13), capital of the Chera kingdom. It was strategically located between the coasts and its growth is thought to relate to the expansion of east coast trade (Champakalakshmi 2006: 103). As already noted, the greatest concentration of Roman coin hoards is from Coimbatore (Fig. 2), primarily Julio-Claudian coins (Turner 1989: 5). The Karur area alone has produced three hoards comprising issues of Augustus, Tiberius and Claudius, as well as individual finds of Hellenistic issue (Turner 1989: 59-60; Krishnamurthy 2000). Additionally *c.* 4,500 Late Roman bronze coins have been collected from Karur and Madurai (Krishnamurthy 2007: 19). From these same sites also come rare Aksumite and imitation Aksumite coins, and from Mangalore a hoard of Aksumite coins of the first half of the fourth century in association with mixed, later Roman ones (Hahn 2000: 287-8, n. 25). Recent excavations at Karur have produced a Roman silver coin and amphorae (Nagaswamy 1995: 62-3) identified as belonging to both Early and Late Roman periods.

At Vellalore a hoard of gold jewellery dated to the first century BC/AD has been attributed to a mixture of Roman and Indian craftsmen (Devasahayam 1985; Nagaswamy 1995: 68). It is difficult to assess the workmanship of the objects from publication alone, but clearly both Classical and Indian themes are represented. A few Tiberian *aurei* were purportedly found alongside the jewellery and other hoards are known from Vellalore (Turner 1989: 81-4). Here, as elsewhere in Tamil Nadu, local artists seem to have been inspired by foreign craftsmen, including those practising Greco-Roman lapidary art (Begley 1996: 29). Begley has compared a well-known first-century intaglio gold ring of a Chera king and queen from Karur with the ceramic intaglio from Arikamedu shown in Fig. 20 (ibid.: 30, fig. 1.15).

Kerala, in Antiquity as today, was the heartland of India's spice-producing area, particularly black pepper. Despite the prominence of Arikamedu and other sites known archaeologically along the Coromandel Coast, it is Kerala's coastline that the Roman documents have emphasised. A number of ports on Limyrike (Malabar Coast) are described in the *Periplus*. Foremost is the Chera port of Muziris, sandwiched between Tyndis to the north and the Pandya twin ports of Bakare/Nelkynda to the south (*PME* 53-5). In the *Periplus* ships routinely dock at Muziris, and although Pliny (*NH* 6.104) calls it '*Primum Emporium Indiae*' he nevertheless advised landing instead at Bakare, down river from Nelkynda.

## 5. Lands to the East

De Romanis has convincingly argued that a preference for Muziris or Bakare can be traced to intertribal disputes between the Chera and the Pandya (De Romanis 1997b: 90-108, esp. 107).

Various locations have been proposed as the site for Muziris, but until recently there was no evidence on the ground. Furthermore, although there are hundreds of Megalithic burials in the area, no Early Historic sites were known in Kerala. An important starting point in the search for Muziris was its association with the Periyar River, named in the *Sangam* poetry:

> ... the flourishing town of Muchiri, where the large beautiful ships built by the Yavanas came with gold, disturbing the white foams of the fair Periyar returned with pepper (*Akam* 149, trans. Zvelebil 1956: 403).

Historically the search for Muziris has centred on the northern banks of the Periyar River and equated Muziris with the adjacent Portuguese fort at Cranganore/Kodungallur (Gurukkal & Whittaker 2001). The lack of Early Historic remains at Kodungallur was attributed to extensive later occupation, but even dredging of the nearby river did not recover any Early Historic finds (Begley 1996: 11, n. 2).

However, this search did not take into account the changing course of the Periyar River visible on satellite imagery, indicating a gradual migration from south to north (Shajan 1998). Thus at *c.* 2000 years BP, when Muziris was active, Kodungallur would not have been located on the Periyar as today. Instead the main channel of the Periyar was at what is now the small stream of the Paravur Thodu (Shajan et al. 2004: fig. 1).

The terrain of Kerala is difficult for archaeological survey because of intensive modern occupation, heavy ground cover and backwaters. Nevertheless, while undertaking geo-

141

archaeological research, K.P. Shajan covered much of the region between Chetwa-Kodungallur-Paravur on foot (ibid.: fig. 1). In doing so he identified an archaeological site at the village of Pattanam associated with Early Historic pottery and other finds. Approximately 1 km south-west of the Paravur Thodu, Pattanam is consistent with the ancient descriptions of Muziris.

Further surface and, in the case of timely modern interventions, subsurface investigation of the site with V. Selvakumar revealed its extensive size, estimated at *c.* 1 km$^2$, and a growing range of artefacts including bricks and beads (Selvakumar et al. 2005). It was at this point, in November 2003, on a visit to Kerala that I was shown the Pattanam pottery and identified an Early Roman amphora, an organic storage jar possibly from Yemen, and Glazed Ware and Torpedo jars of uncertain date from Mesopotamia. Furthermore, among the CRSW were sherds with the distinctive internal wiping marks seen at Berenike and Myos Hormos, but not elsewhere in India outside Kerala.

A convincing argument for equating Pattanam with Muziris was being constructed (Shajan et al. 2004), but additional investigation was needed. An opportunity for controlled excavation arose in 2004 and two trenches established by Hill Palace Museum allowed the definition of three cultural phases including Iron Age-Early Historic transition (Megalithic); Early Historic (overseas trade contact phase) and Early Medieval (Selvakumar et al. 2005; Selvakumar et al. in press). The sequence demonstrated that, as at Arikamedu, the site was operative before the overseas contact period dated between approximately the late first century BC and third century AD. Brick architecture, together with the quantity and variety of finds (including amphorae and Italian *sigillata*), established its urban character and reinforced its connection with Muziris (Shajan et al. 2008).

## 5. Lands to the East

More extensive excavation conducted by P.J. Cherian, for the Kerala Council for Historical Research, and the Archaeological Survey of India in spring 2007 and 2008, is building up a more comprehensive picture of the site, including the identification of an Early Historic wooden wharf and boat (reported on by Nair 2008). Additional finds should refine the period for Western contact. A survey of the site by Abraham (2005) will help to contextualise the excavation trenches within the larger site. Cosmas Indicopleustes (*Topography* 11.16) mentions the Male (Malabar) Coast as the source of pepper, but does not list Muziris as one of the ports (Gurukkal & Whittaker 2001: 338); from this we may infer that by the mid-sixth century it no longer functioned.

Its role as a transhipment centre, as described in the Muziris papyrus (Rathbone 2001) and the *Sangam* poetry (De Romanis 1997b: 94-5), is verified by finds from elsewhere in India including beads from the Coimbatore region. The Muziris papyrus specifically mentions Gangetic nard and textiles, both organics and therefore poorly preserved, but imports from the same region can be traced by more tangible items from eastern India, such as RW and Paddle Impressed Wares.

Four coin hoards are recorded from the vicinity of Pattanam: Roman ones from Iyyal, Valluvalli and Kumbalam extending into the second century and a punch-marked one from Puthenchira (Sathyamurthy 1992: 4-5; Gurukkal 1989: 160). The Iyyal hoard is exceptional in containing both gold and silver issues (up to Trajan), as well as silver punch-marked ones (Sathyamurthy 1992: 4; Turner 1989: 55). We have already noted the linking of foreigners and gold in the *Sangam* literature, which resonates in this area rich in Roman coins.

The discovery of Pattanam not only provides a convincing location on the ground for Muziris, but, as the first Early Historic settlement in Kerala, enables the relationship between the Malabar and Coromandel Coasts to be explored.

143

We have already traced communication between the coasts through the exchange of artefacts. Two main routes existed for this exchange. One was by sea, hugging Cape Comorin, for which *PME* 59 describes the site at Komar as a stopping point; by the time of Ptolemy it was a city (Casson 1989: 224-5; *Geography* 7.1.9). The most accessible land route was through a break in the Western Ghats known as Palghat Gap, which, as today, connected the coasts. There are few excavated archaeological sites or finds from Cape Comorin itself; in contrast the land route is marked by numerous Megalithic sites (Rajan 1994: 178-9) and Roman coins (MacDowall 1998: figs 4, 8 and 9). Coins on the land route may reflect the nature of the region, rich in mineral resources that were exchanged, while the coastal route can be seen as a quick means by which to reach the east coast trade, not by Roman ships but in small, local boats (*PME* 60). Turner has argued that the second-century coins from the mouth of the Krishna area demonstrate intensification of the east coast and support rounding of the Cape during this period (1989: 5). This is in keeping with the greater detail of Ptolemy (Tripathi 2002: 118), which is matched by the *Sangam* texts (Champakalakshmi 2006: 179-80) and also correlated with the Satavahana shift from the western Deccan to the lower Krishna Valley (Ray 1996: 356).

## Sri Lanka: Mantai, Anuradhapura and Tissamaharama (Figs 19 and 21)

Modern Sri Lanka, or Taprobane to the Greeks and Romans, was strategically located as a commercial interface between China and the West (the Indian subcontinent, Mediterranean, Persia, Arabia). Its cultural history merits a fuller treatment than can be given here. More detail regarding Sri Lanka during the Greco-Roman period is provided by Weerakkody (1997) and in site-specific reports referred to below. Here exchange patterns, which, as outlined by Bopearachchi, were intimately connected with India, are emphasised (1997: xv-xix). During the proto-historic or Megalithic period, material culture – particularly ceramics and including RW – suggests close association with South India. By legend its Early Historic period was heralded by merchant settlers from North India, and the second phase, visible archaeologically, by the introduction of Buddhism through an envoy of the Mauryan king Ashoka. The strength of association with North India is reflected by Indian punch-marked coins and subsequently Indo-Greek, Indo-Scythian, Indo-Parthian and Kushana ones. From the first century AD, Pandya coins in Sri Lanka reflect commercial connections with South India. For much of its ancient history, the treacherous waters of the Gulf of Mannar and Adam's Bridge provided the link between India and Sri Lanka (Bopearachchi 1992: 62).

Coins are the most prolific Roman find in Sri Lanka, but here the comparison with India ends. Only a handful of Early Imperial coins have been recovered, in contrast to the over 200,000 'third brass' and Indo-Roman imitations dating to the fourth and fifth centuries found particularly on the west coast (Bopearachchi 1997: xvii, xix; 1998: 70).

The most detailed description of Taprobane comes from Ptolemy (*Geography* 7.4); recognition of its international importance from Cosmas (*Topography* 11.13-15), who recounts that ships arrived at the central trade harbour, in the north of the island, from India, Persia and Ethiopia. In support, a number of Sasanian coins have also been collected on the island (Bopearachchi 1998: 71-2), and rare Aksumite ones (see below). Although important as a transhipment centre, Sri Lanka was inherently wealthy, including the 'hyacinth stone' from the southern kingdom, which may refer to sapphire or other gemstones (Carswell ibid.; Weerakkody 1997: 136).

Three sites are exceptional for imported finds from

excavated Early Historic sites: Mantai, Anuradhapura and Tissamaharama. In the northern kingdom, Anuradhapura would have been linked by the Aruvi Ari River to the island's main port at Mantai, and it is Mantai that Cosmas most likely described as the main harbour (Carswell 1990: 25-6). The most recent excavations at Mantai comprised three seasons between 1980 and 1984; the surface and excavated finds demonstrate its importance between the Mesolithic period and the tenth century AD (Carswell & Prickett 1984; Carswell 1990), including sherds identified as Italian and West Asian *sigillata* (Silva 1985: 46).

The interior site of Anuradhapura, the Sinhalese royal capital, has been more extensively excavated and a sequence from the fifth century BC to AD 1100 proposed (Coningham 2006: table 1.1). The most prolific imports at Anuradhapura come from Mesopotamia, mostly of Sasanian and Early Islamic date. These comprise Torpedo jars and Glazed Ware (Coningham & Batt 1999: 129; Seely et al. 2006: 99), which were also present at Mantai, as were other Sasanian finds including a Persian inscription, a Nestorian cross and a clay *bulla* (Carswell 1990: 26; Carswell & Prickett 1984: 64, table 1; Prickett-Fernando 1990: 68). Other Western finds excavated from Anuradhapura include five Late Roman bronze coins (Bopearachchi 2006: 13) and five fragments of Eastern Mediterranean glass dating between the first centuries BC and AD (Coningham 2006: 334-5).

On the south coast, excavations at Tissamaharama (Mahagama, the ancient capital of Ruhuna) provide interesting imported material. It is judged that in Antiquity Tissamaharama, located *c.* 10 km from the sea, was connected to a coastal port by the Kirindi Oya River (H. Schenk, pers. comm.). Nevertheless, it was a major port in its own right from around 400 BC, with a decline after AD 500. Again, a concentration of Torpedo jars from the Sasanian and Early

Islamic periods is recorded, as is Glazed Ware from contexts dating between the Parthian and Islamic periods (Schenk 2001: 74, in press). Roman finds, however, are more prolific here than at Anuradhapura. These include Early and Late Roman amphorae, and over 470 coins from the region. Over 40 coins, primarily of fourth- and fifth-century date, have been excavated at the site, as has an Aksumite one and an Egyptian imitation of an Aksumite coin (Walburg 2001, 2008: 54). The presence of Torpedo jars, beginning in the Sasanian period, correlates well with Cosmas, who alongside the Roman emphasises the Sasanian role in the trade of Taprobane (*Topography* 11.13-19).

## Trade and traders

Most of the sites discussed here were situated on trade routes, were religious or of secular importance. Where known, many had phases predating the Roman contact period that reinforce the importance of pre-existing trade routes in the spread of Roman artefacts. At Arikamedu the use of Megalithic pottery both before and after the introduction of traded Western goods indicates the continuing importance of the local population (Begley 1996: 18). The role of existing internal trade routes would have varied throughout India, for exchange was particularly well-developed in the Deccan and spread through Buddhist monasteries, while in the South religious structures denoting participation in trade networks have not been recognised (Abraham 2007: 289). Roman exchange attached itself to indigenous systems, especially for subsistence items, with their established framework for procuring and disposing of goods (Ray 1995b: 98, 1998: 188). This would have increased the demand for spices, raw materials and manufactured items and stimulated these pre-existing networks, but the full impact of this demand –

147

for instance whether it encouraged urbanism – is unknown (Abraham 2007: 293-4).

Ray has summarised textual evidence, including inscriptions from throughout India and the *Arthashastra*, *Jatakas* and *Sangam* poems, to build up a picture of how trade and merchants were organised (1988: 36-40). Her overall consensus is that most trade was conducted privately, but provided revenue for the ruling elite. Chronological and geographical variations would have existed, with the regional elite, for example, sometimes taking a role in price setting and the production of trade items (Jahan 2005: 81; see also Seland 2006: 154-6, 186).

Trade was conducted by both Indians and foreigners. Casson argues that at Barygaza, import-export was most likely handled by local merchants, in contrast to Muziris/Nelkynda where there was 'unmistakable' evidence for a resident foreign colony (1989: 24). This last conclusion was derived firstly from the Temple of Augustus on the Peutinger Table, secondly from the Muziris papyrus, which Casson believes was written in India, and finally from the implication in *PME* 56 that grain was imported for foreigners but not locals at Muziris/Nelkynda. The Temple of Augustus as a real edifice has already been largely discounted (Chapter 2, p. 30). Evidence from the two documents is more compelling, but is still open to interpretation (Seland 2007b: 78). Regardless of where the Muziris papyrus was drawn up, it seems clear that foreigners were resident at Muziris, although it was not a colonial station. They would have had to stay, even if only while trade was conducted and ships were unloaded and provisioned for their return journey (ibid.: 79). Thus the Muziris community was heterogeneous, also including non-local Indian traders from the north-west (*PME* 54; De Romanis 1997b: 94).

Wheeler assumed that there was a Roman colony at Arikamedu. Meyer has summarised the Coromandel sites in the *Periplus*, noting that no exports, but only imports from Limyrike, are itemised – a treatment that is similar to the Gulf (2007: 63). He argues that trade with the east coast was indirect, and was not conducted by Romans, as concluded above for West Bengal. Yet as we learn more, the similarities between Pattanam and Arikamedu increase. It follows that if Romans were at least temporarily resident at Muziris, the same applies at Arikamedu. In this respect, does the concentration of Greek amphorae in the Northern Sector of Arikamedu (Begley 2004c: 114) have any significance? Does it imply that foreign merchants were segregated within that site, or merely an area where amphorae exchanged hands? To address these questions, the individual find spots need to be evaluated: for example, were they from primary or secondary contexts? Language and familiarity with local customs would, at least initially, have been a barrier to foreign traders. In some places during medieval times, foreign traders were ghettoised, excluded from local markets and made dependent upon local middlemen (Ray 1985: 19). Elsewhere, though, as implied by the Deccan cave inscriptions, foreign traders integrated themselves within the local merchant community.

Westerners in India required amphora-borne products to maintain their Roman lifestyle, but the local residents might also have consumed these foods. From Wheeler onwards the *Sangam* reference to 'cool fragrant wine brought by the *Yavanas*' (*Puram* 50, trans. Zvelebil 1956: 402) has been cited in support of Indian's taste for wine (Wheeler et al. 1946: 21). Kashmir had the climate most suitable for cultivation and in the seventh century the Chinese Buddhist Xuan Zang mentions grape growing brought from Kashmir (Achaya 1994: 148). Other alcoholic drinks were fermented and distilled in India so a taste for alcoholic beverages was widespread (Menon 1970: 82-3). *Purananuru* 343 notes that 'toddy is no more valuable than water' to the king of Muziris (trans. Hart &

Heifetz 1999: 196). In his *History of Alexander the Great* (8.9.30), written from secondary sources during the first century AD, Quintus Curtius describes an Indian king: 'Women prepare his food. They also serve his wine, the use of which is lavish with all the Indian peoples.' In direct contrast the early fifth-century Chinese Buddhist Fa Xian writes 'Throughout the country no one kills any living thing, nor drinks wine ...' (Achaya 1994: 147). These opposing quotations reflect an uneven attitude to alcohol over time. Social status may also have been a factor (Karttunen 1989: 209), with wine-drinking associated with the urban elite (Ray 1998: 70). Will has suggested that wines held in Koan or Koan-style amphorae (Dressel 2-4), made with salt water, were the most agreeable to the Indian palate (2004: 328-31). Arikamedu is the only site where Koan amphorae constitute a large proportion of the assemblage. Given the difficulty in identifying them, their quantity may be slightly overestimated; nevertheless at present the findings are unparalleled elsewhere in India.

Amphorae for *garum* and oil are much less common in India than those for wine. With its salty taste, *garum* is comparable to fish sauce produced using similar techniques and now consumed in quantity throughout Southeast Asia (Curtis 2001: 409). Although fish sauce was not eaten in India, salted fish were available in Tamilakam and elsewhere (Achaya 2002: 70), so there may well have been a taste for it in Antiquity. Olive oil is more difficult to evaluate, but other oils, including fish oil, are and were used in India (Achaya 1994: 50). Regardless of whether Indians had a positive liking for imported foodstuffs, their acquisition would have carried status.

Tangible evidence that imported goods were in Indian hands is provided by a sherd of *sigillata* from Arikamedu with a Tamil-Brahmi graffito (Begley 1996: 22; Comfort 1992: 141, fig. 8.13). At both Arikamedu (Will 2004: 324, n. 1) and Tissamaharama some amphora sherds were reused, as identified by their smoothed edges. While this selection for reuse may relate to the highly visible nature of these sherds and their durable (hard-fired) quality, it also suggests a degree of choice related to their scarcity.

A situation analogous to the Indian one existed for trade conducted between Britain and Gaul prior to the Roman conquest, and Whitehouse has drawn parallels between Camulodunum (pre-Roman Colchester) and Arikamedu. At Camulodunum a small amount of imported amphorae, *sigillata* and glass may represent the needs of a resident foreign (Roman) community (Whitehouse 1990: 490). Another Iron Age parallel comes from Welwyn in Hertfordshire, where imported Roman amphorae, silver cups and ceramic cups and plates were excavated from the graves of wealthy non-Romans (Potter & Johns 2002: 128, 138).

# 6

# Changing scenes and forces

It is clear from the preceding chapters that new evidence challenges and enhances older interpretations of Indo-Roman trade. The range and quantity of Roman and non-Roman goods involved are enlarged and the timeframe better understood. Even its shorthand 'Roman' oversimplifies the contribution of different ethnic groups to transoceanic exchange. In this study 'Roman' has been used as an umbrella term for different ethnic groups who resided within the Empire. Nevertheless, actual Romans were also involved. Tchernia has brought together inscriptional evidence from Egypt's Eastern Desert and a stamped amphora from Mathura to show that the Italian *Peticius* family was directly involved in the supply of amphorae to India (1997a). Another Eastern Desert inscription confirms the participation of the *Annii* family of Puteoli (Tchernia 1997a: 239; De Romanis 1997a: 167-71).

Embassies between India and the West were known from Hellenistic/Mauryan times, and Ptolemy II received one (Hourani 1995: 23; Thapar 1997: 19). Others were exchanged between India and the Roman Empire during the period between Augustus and Justinian, and diplomatic contacts were maintained with Ethiopia and South Arabia until the seventh century (Sidebotham 1996b: 299 for references). These interchanges underline the status of Roman interests in the Indian Ocean and the need for their diplomatic goodwill, rather than Imperial control (Sidebotham 1986: 129-30, 178; Casson 1989: 38). Imperial interest and profit, as opposed to control, is

152

indicated more by the imposition of the 25% state importation tax. Nevertheless, evidence from documents, sites and finds all point to the Roman component of trade being undertaken by private individuals. The enormous cost and complexity of the undertaking would not have precluded private enterprise, but did preclude small merchants acting on their own; instead extremely wealthy merchants or a consortia of merchants would have been required to finance the ventures (Whittaker 2004: 169). The Muziris papyrus implies a hierarchy in which a wealthy financier recruited merchants to undertake the trips (Rathbone 2001: 43).

We have seen that each of our regions was involved to some degree, as attested by the presence of foreign residents at many ports during both the Early and Late Roman period. Their presence can be detected textually, and archaeologically by graffiti of diverse linguistic groups and imported items that may represent personal possessions, whose use was identified with a particular ethnic group. Foreign residents probably comprised both merchants and sailors, although the two cannot be distinguished archaeologically. As aliens they would have united into communities due to 'common bonds of language, customs, religion and occupation' (Sidebotham 1996b: 299).

Clearly there was some mingling between these groups, but it is difficult to assess whether they collaborated on the same voyage or acted separately. *PME* 26 indicates that Indian ships sailed to the Red Sea (Casson 1989: 20). Indian sails and timbers found on the Red Sea coast (Vermeeren 2000: 340-1; Wild & Wild 2001) seemingly provide the tangible evidence for this; technology transfer between Indians and Romans may also have played its part, just as diffusion can be seen from locally produced Roman-style artefacts in India.

In this chapter we move from a geographical framework to a diachronic one, in order to bring together the evidence described in Chapters 3-5 and evaluate the changing nature of long-distance exchange. The chronological periods are broadly divided into 'Early' and 'Late' Roman in order to create larger datasets and highlight the geographical and chronological distinctions.

Since the emphasis is on pottery it is appropriate to say a few words about reuse, which may inflect distribution patterns. Two very distinct kinds of reuse are obvious from Egypt – most dramatically the jetty at Myos Hormos (front cover), and from Berenike written instructions to decant local wine into a foreign amphora (Bagnall et al. 2000: 18). Sedov has suggested that a similar reuse took place at Qana, where Dressel 2-4 amphorae were filled with Arabian wine and then exported to India (2007: 102). There is no consistent methodology for recognising this process, but since lined, local Organic Storage Jars suitable for this purpose are commonly found in Egypt, and occasionally in India, there was no pressing need for reuse on a large scale. Within India reuse of Roman amphorae may have occurred, perhaps as gift exchange, and this may be the explanation for single occurrences of imported amphorae.

### The Early Roman period (first century BC to third century AD)

Between the late first century BC and the mid-third century AD there is Roman activity at the Red Sea ports for economically motivated Indian Ocean trade. Berenike, Marsa Nakari, Myos Hormos, Clysma and Aila were all active. It is paradoxical that during the Early Roman period when Indian Ocean trade was intense, the main trade ports lacked substantial infrastructure, which may provide another argument against Imperial control.

During this period Myos Hormos and Berenike belonged to a Mediterranean trading network, connected through Alexandria. Most supplies would have arrived via the Nile,

although those from Nabataea may have arrived either by the
Red Sea or by land, and others such as Mesopotamian Glazed
Ware via Palmyra. Trajan's Canal may also have played a role
in bringing provisions from the Nile (Sidebotham 1996b: 292).
Aila, on the other hand, owed its existence to the incense trade,
and its overland connections are reflected in ceramic
assemblages that look particularly to the Levant (S.T. Parker
2002: 424-5). Relations between Nabataea and the East would
have included an overland leg by caravan, hinted at by the
possible Indian moulded vessel found at Petra (Gogte 1999).

Myos Hormos and Berenike also differ from Aila in terms of
Indian finds, which are plentiful in Egypt. Indian ceramic
imports that can be sourced are dominated by those from the
south and east coasts, with an apparent decrease in the second
century. However, Rouletted Ware could also have travelled
from the east coast via the north-west port of Barygaza
(Schenk in press); pepper, gems and glass beads reinforce the
importance of South India during this period, as do the few
Tamil- and Prakrit-Brahmi graffiti (Mahadevan 1996, 2007;
Salomon 1991). The Muziris papyrus makes clear that
products from elsewhere in India, such as Gangetic nard, were
distributed via entrepots, of which Muziris was of prime
importance. Further support comes from the Keralan
organically gouged CRSW found in Egypt. Elsewhere in the
Indian Ocean it is difficult to trace this distinctive type since
manufacturing techniques are not published. Organic Black
Ware from Gujarat is easier to trace by shape and has been
identified at Aila, Myos Hormos and Berenike, but not in South
India. This could indicate direct contact with the North,
possibly through Barygaza, but this must be balanced against
the corresponding absence of Gujarati RPW at Red Sea sites.
At the same time, the source of some CRSW found in Egypt is
unknown and could come from central or North India.

Rare RPW at Qana, Khor Rori and possibly Mleiha, and

Organic Black Ware at Khor Rori and Qana (see Table 2; Sedov 2007; Sedov & Benvenuti 2002; Benoist et al. 2003) may indicate stopovers in South Arabia between North India and the Red Sea. Additionally, South Arabia-India routes may have existed separately from the Red Sea (see below). The forthcoming final publication on Qana may allow a more informed quantitative assessment of Organic Black Ware, which will enhance our understanding of the region. Continuing down the Red Sea, some connections between the Roman world and Adulis and Aksum can be drawn, but were fairly undeveloped during this period.

In India the distribution of Roman luxury objects, such as metalwork and intaglios, was rare, with relatively more found in the north. Larger categories of finds, coins and pottery, are more informative and like luxury items respected coastal and inland trade routes. Previous distribution maps of Roman amphorae indicated a concentration in Gujarat and at Arikamedu (Ray 2003) and that concentration is still visible if all amphorae are viewed together (Fig. 21). By separating Early and Late Roman ones and distinguishing them from Mesopotamian Torpedo jars, this effect is lessened, particularly for the Early Roman period. Early Roman amphorae are more widely dispersed with clustering in the far south. The largest assemblages are at Arikamedu and Pattanam, the next largest at Nevasa; otherwise distribution is thin, occurring as 1-3 sherds, but with a steady trickle reported from ongoing excavations.

The Campanian wine amphora is the single most common type throughout the Indian Ocean. In part this reflects the ease with which the clay fabric can be identified, but also the quantity of Campanian vessels travelling from west to east between the late first century BC and the first century AD, and the magnitude of the Campanian wine industry before the eruption of Vesuvius in AD 79. The dominance of Campanian amphorae in first-century deposits at Myos Hormos and Berenike correlates with evidence from the Berenike *ostraca* for the shipment of Italian wine to India (Bagnall et al. 2000: 16-21).

Early Roman amphorae from both the Western and Eastern Mediterranean have been identified in India and on a reduced scale reflect trends seen throughout the Mediterranean (Fig. 3). In aggregate the sources of Roman amphorae in India comprise a slightly wider range than is published from elsewhere in the Indian Ocean, e.g. Qana and Khor Rori, but can be matched at Alexandria and at the Egyptian sites. Further research may alter these patterns, but at present this distribution supports some direct voyages between Egypt and particularly South India, where the greatest diversity in amphora sources is seen. Direct voyages are also indicated by the presence of Indian residents, and the large quantity of Indian pottery found on the Egyptian Red Sea sites, but not penetrating further into the Roman world.

*Natural History* 6.96-104 is a key passage where Pliny described in chronological order various routes employed from the time of Alexander to the present. Previously they set sail from South Arabia to northern India, but now 'it will not be amiss to set out the whole of the voyage from Egypt' [to Muziris] (*NH* 6.101), but from Okelis on the coast of Arabia Felix one finds 'the most advantageous way of sailing' (*NH* 6.104; Tchernia 1997b: 251; De Romanis 1997b: 85-9). So there were two ways to reach Muziris/Limyrike, direct and indirect.

How breaks affected cargo composition may have been influenced by the length of the stay, which in turn was influenced by weather and wind conditions. For instance, Rougé has proposed that sometimes Roman ships spent several weeks at Qana in order to fit in with wind regimes (Salles 2005: 264; Rougé 1988). If the break was short local products may have been added to the hold of a not quite full ship; longer stays may have required the complete unloading of the ship, whose initial cargo could then be radically transformed when it eventually left harbour. The *Periplus* suggests, for example, that only incense and Arabian wine were added to ships travelling between Egypt and India (Casson 1989: 21). Archaeological recognition of these different processes is frustratingly difficult and, as will be seen below, alternative explanations can frequently account for artefact distribution.

As described in the *Periplus*, itineraries existed independently of those between Rome-India and Arabia-India, particularly routes to Africa. These were shorter, some even local, took less time and investment and therefore could be undertaken by smaller-scale traders (Casson 1989: 291; Salles 1993: 507). Journeys between Egypt and Qana, but not necessarily Khor Rori, are suggested by ceramic and basalt finds. The outward route from the Red Sea is manifested by the large and diverse Roman ceramic assemblages at Qana and Khor Rori, particularly amphorae (Sedov 2007; Sedov & Benvenuti 2002). The return can be reconstructed from pottery and basalt finds at Myos Hormos and Berenike, which for both include small numbers of finds from the region of Aden and much larger quantities from the Hadramawt. This closed trip would have catered to the incense trade and the basalt, particularly, provided suitable ballast for ships whose main cargo was frankincense (Peacock et al. 2007: 62). Furthermore, it correlates well with Sedov's hypothesis that during the Lower period Qana served mainly as a small port for Egypt (2007: 104-5).

Subsistence items were a major export from India to Arabia and the Gulf (Gupta 2007). The journey between India and Arabia can be traced by the robust Indian ceramic assemblages at both Qana and Khor Rori (Sedov 2007; Sedov & Benvenuti 2002). Trips between South Arabia and India could have provided a mechanism for the transhipment of Roman amphorae to India, as well as the rare sherds of Organic Storage Jars identified at Pattanam and Arikamedu; but both could also result from a stopover between the Red Sea and India. Gupta visualises an alternative situation, whereby Roman ships returning to the Red Sea from India with subsistence goods stopped at South Arabia and exchanged these subsistence items for frankincense (2007: esp. 117).

The position of the Gulf within this early trade network is highlighted by the ceramic assemblages from Ras Hafun/Opone, where Roman pottery is common and Mesopotamian pottery moderate to rare (Smith & Wright 1988). This is in stark contrast to the Gulf sites where Mesopotamian and Roman ceramics occur together, but Roman ones are rare and probably arrived indirectly either overland or via Qana (Rutten 2007: 19; Tomber 2007b: 983).

At Ras Hafun, Egyptian and Mediterranean wares were common during the first century and absent by the second/third century. Mesopotamian wares and sparse Indian types occur in both assemblages. The sizeable quantities of Roman and Mesopotamian wares may reflect its function as a meeting point for Roman and Persian merchants during the first century, for, according to *PME* 13, slaves were exported to Egypt and elsewhere from Opone (Groom 1995: 189). Equally, direct journeys from Ras Hafun to both Egypt and the head of the Gulf would account for the assemblages. The absence of Roman material after the first century signals a change in relations with the Roman world and contrasts with Ptolemy's detailed second-century description of East Africa.

Opone was a redistribution point, not only for slaves, but for rice (Cappers 2006: 104-5). The limited quantity of Asian ceramics at Ras Hafun suggests indirect supply and supports the premise that the East African route was separate from India at this time (Smith & Wright 1988: 139). Most of the Indian imports cannot be precisely sourced, with Organic

Black Ware an exception. No single all-embracing explanation accounts for these short journeys, but they uphold the idea of separate regional itineraries introduced in the *Periplus*. Like Gupta (2007: 115) we support the active input of all the different groups: Romans, Arabs, Persians, Africans and Indians.

The relationship between amphorae and subsistence commodities is well known, but pottery other than transport containers also travelled. Egyptian coarse wares (jars, bowls and jugs) are unlikely to have been exported systematically and may have been the personal possessions of sailors and merchants. They should therefore have special potential for understanding routes between Egypt and India. Unfortunately at present their recognition may be uneven and their distribution pattern outside Egypt unreliable.

Similarly the distribution of Roman and Indian fine wares throughout the Indian Ocean is of interest, for they occur in small numbers and the Roman ones are more restricted than amphorae from the same region. Additional data is required to explore these differences and more generally investigate the mechanisms accounting for their distribution. To this end some key pottery types are tabulated on Table 2 to illustrate the distribution of non-amphora types. *Sigillata* were recorded on all the sites except Ras Hafun, which supports Smith and Wright's view that it was a temporary encampment (1988: 139). The occurrence of Roman glass in association with fine wares warrants further consideration, but is beyond the scope of this book. Of particular interest are sites where imported glass is more common than pottery, such as Heis (Stern 1993), and the Gulf sites of Mleiha, Ed Dur and Dibba (Jassim 2006; Whitehouse 1998, 2000), where much of the first-century glass was found in burial contexts.

| Site | Sigillata | Roman Glazed Ware | Roman Table Ware | Indian RW | Indian RPW | Indian Organic Black Ware | Indian Other Coarse Wares |
|---|---|---|---|---|---|---|---|
| Myos Hormos | ✓ | ✓ | ✓ | ✓ | | ✓ | ✓ |
| Berenike | ✓ | ✓ | ✓ | ✓ | | ✓ | ✓ |
| Adulis | ✓ | | | | | | |
| Aksum | ✓ | | | | | | |
| Hafun | | | | | | ✓ | ✓ |
| Qana | ✓ | | ✓ | ✓ | ✓ | ✓ | ✓ |
| Khor Rori | ✓ | | | | ✓ | ✓ | ✓ |
| Timna | ✓ | ✓ | | | | | |
| Shabwa | ✓ | | ✓ | | | | |
| Ed Dur | ✓ | | | | | | |
| Mleiha | ✓ | | | | ? | | ✓ |
| Pattanam | ✓ | | | ✓ | | | ✓ |
| Arikamedu | ✓ | | | ✓ | | | ✓ |
| Alagankulam | ✓ | | | ✓ | | | ✓ |

Table 2. Pottery types from Indian Ocean sites during the Early Roman period.

## The Late Roman/Byzantine period (fourth to early/mid-seventh century AD)

After a dip in occupation from the mid-third century, the fourth century sees rejuvenation on the Red Sea coast, with chronological indicators particularly strong from the mid-fourth century. In the Roman/Byzantine world the Arab conquest marks the disruption of trade routes and the end of Roman involvement.

Ray (1998: 67) has drawn attention to Raschke's (1975: 244-5) observations, that there are more Egyptian textual references to Indian spices in the third and fourth centuries than earlier. In the Red Sea, Aila and Clysma were well established, there was a resurgence of occupation at Berenike, Abu Shaar was founded and small-scale excavations at Marsa Nakari also indicate occupation during this period. The

161

transformation of the Aksumite kingdom into an international power is evident from its capital at Aksum and its port at Adulis. Fifth-century deposits are also identified from Ras Hafun. Generally, except for Hafun, these sites are more substantial and more complex during this period when Indo-Roman trade was previously thought to be greatly reduced. At Adulis, for example, decorative marbles from throughout the Roman world were used for church decoration (Munro-Hay 1989b). Berenike flourished with a grid system (Sidebotham 2002: 227) and a town wall was built at Aila (Parker: 2000: 392), although this was probably due to security issues rather than investment in trade *per se* (Ward 2007).

Greater uniformity existed not only between the northern and southern Roman Red Sea, but beyond the Roman world. This is observable particularly by the distribution of Aqaba amphorae at Aila, Abu Shaar, Marsa Nakari, Berenike, Adulis, Aksum and other sites in Ethiopia. Beyond the Red Sea they are found at Qana and Shabwa and in growing numbers from India (Tomber 2004a; Ballet & Lemaître forthcoming). Importantly none have been found in Alexandria. Apart from the Iskandil Burnu shipwreck off Turkey (Lloyd 1985), all occurrences of Aqaba amphorae are associated with sites within the Indian Ocean trade region. Their content is not firmly established, with two schools of thought – that they were containers for fish products from the environs of Aila (Parker 2000: 380), or alternatively for wine or date products (Peacock 2007a: 104). In support of wine, an Aqaba sherd from Berenike had an inscription reading *oinos* (Tomber 2004a: 398, not date wine as reported by Dolinka 2003: 95). Aila, Clysma, Berenike and Adulis are further united in the *Martyrium Sancti Arethae*. From this text we know that in AD 524-5, of the 70 ships gathered at Adulis to aid the Aksumite invasion of King Kaleb to South Arabia, 20 came from Clysma, 15 from Aila, 10 from

## 6. Changing scenes and forces

Adulis and two from Berenike, as well as 9 from India and 7 from Farasan (Glazier & Peacock 2007: 10, 128).

The introduction of Aksumite coinage in the late third century makes the dispersion of Aksumite culture much more visible than earlier; also the growing importance of the kingdom meant that more artefacts were in circulation. Coins included not only genuine Aksumite ones, but their moulded imitations likely to have been produced in Egypt. Imitations are more common in the Roman world than the genuine ones (Hahn 1994-9: 106), but a single genuine one was excavated from Berenike (Sidebotham 2007: 201). Although not securely provenanced, Aksumite coins are more commonly found in the Levant during Late Roman or Early Islamic times and are associated with Christian pilgrimage sites, including Aila, which may have been the entry point for them (Hahn 1994-9, 2004: 286). Away from the Roman world there is a sprinkling of hoards, and genuine and imitation coins found in South Arabia, South India and Sri Lanka (Tomber 2005b; Walburg 2008: 54).

Despite the unprepossessing appearance of undecorated Aksumite sherds, making them hard to identify, both undecorated and decorated ones have been recorded outside Aksumite contexts. On the Red Sea sites they are most plentiful at Berenike; significantly fewer have been identified at Aila. Although they may be underestimated at Aila, it remains, as earlier, distinct from Berenike by the substantially fewer imports from East Africa, the Hadramawt and India.

Aksumite sherds are fairly common from the late Middle and Upper period at Qana, attributed to the strong political ties with the Aksumite realm (Sedov 1998: 28). Thus, the brisk interchange of artefacts seen between Qana and Aksum is not surprising, but is, significantly, visible in only one direction. The most distant occurrence of Aksumite pottery is a sherd from recent excavations at Kamrej in Gujarat (Tomber 2005a).

163

The restricted Aila finds suggest it was a place of export rather than import. Contact between Aksum/Adulis and Aila was probably indirect, through Berenike or, later, Clysma, although the archaeological evidence for Clysma is lacking. In this context the co-occurrence of Aksumite coins and Aqaba amphorae at Berenike, Qana, and Shabwa is noted (see above; Sedov & 'Aydarus 1995: 53; Tomber 2005b), but the proposed role of Aila in the distribution of Aksumite coins to pilgrimage sites should be borne in mind.

Traditionally, Late Roman activity in Indian Ocean trade is thought to be via Aksumite and Himyarite middlemen (Sidebotham 1986: 46-7). From South Arabia the only visible marker we have is the Organic Storage Jar, which ceased production at the latest by the early fifth century AD. The cessation of Khor Rori and the reduction in Indian wares at Qana between the Middle and Upper periods may, however, reflect a decline of the Indian-Arabian leg and the Himyarite contribution to trade. Conversely, for Aksum, the increase in Aksumite finds at Berenike, and a shared material culture between the two Red Sea powers, supports their role as middlemen. However, the level of Roman involvement remained substantial enough to warrant increased infrastructure at Berenike and highlights the ongoing investment and Roman participation in Indian Ocean commerce. The relatively few Aksumite finds in India are likely to increase substantially as they become better understood and more readily identified. At present they contrast sharply with the more common Roman finds, and suggest that while assisted particularly by Aksumite middlemen, the Romans still provided the impetus for commerce with the East.

This is further emphasised by the minimal presence of Indian finds in the Late Roman period in East Africa, as compared to Berenike, despite textual references to ships travelling from India to East Africa and Indian ships named in the *Martyrium Sancti Arethae* (Walburg 2008: 234-8). At Aksum, archaeobotanical studies by Boardman and Gale (2000) did not identify pepper. This may relate to preservation and availability (see below), or its absence may reflect a different palate from the Roman one. Another item, Indo-Pacific beads, travelled to Matara and Aksum in the interior of Ethiopia (Harlow 2000; Anfray & Annequin 1965: pl clv b).

Many Late Roman contexts at Berenike are difficult to assess given problems of residuality, but the finds from Shenshef, with its fifth/sixth century foundation, demonstrates continued importation during this period. South India appears the most important, both for southern goods and as a transhipment point for Sri Lanka, while the fourth century coin of Rudrasena III from Berenike suggests some continued input from further north (Sidebotham 2007: 201). At present it seems that by the Late Roman period Muziris/Pattanam had declined and been overtaken by other ports on the Malabar Coast: Parti, Mangarouth (Mangalore), Salopatanan, Nalopatana and Poudopatana are mentioned by Cosmas in the sixth century (*Topography* 11.15-16; McCrindle 1897: nn. 3-4).

The distribution of Late Roman coins in India is informative and contrasts with the early ones, particularly in the dominance of bronze. These occur in Gujarat, along the Ganges, in Uttar Pradesh, with concentrations in South India at Madurai and Karur, and in Sri Lanka (Fig. 2). Late Roman amphorae cluster in the north, from Gujarat and Maharashtra with only rare sherds from Arikamedu and Karur, and Tissamaharama in Sri Lanka (Fig. 21). By tabulating the late amphora types (Table 3), the potential routes are clarified.

Within the Late Roman timeframe two phases can be distinguished by the presence or absence of the Aegean LR2, which was widely distributed from the mid-late fifth century and was produced until at least the mid-seventh century. The absence of LR2 at Berenike, last mentioned in the *Martyrium*

| Type | India | Alexandria | Aila | Berenike | Hafun Main | Adulis | Aksum | Qana |
|---|---|---|---|---|---|---|---|---|
| LR1 | Arikamedu Bharuch? Elephanta Hathab Kamrej Kateshwar? Prabhas-Somnath | ✓ | ✓ | ✓ | | ✓ | ✓ | ✓ |
| LR2 | Elephanta | ✓ | | | | ✓ | | |
| LR3 | Ajabpura | ✓ | ✓ | ✓ | | ✓ | ✓ | |
| LR4 | | ✓ | ✓ | ✓ | | | | ✓ |
| LR7 | Elephanta | ✓ | ✓ | ✓ | | | | |
| Aqaba amphorae | Elephanta Kamrej Kateshwar Nagara | | ✓ | ✓ | | ✓ | ✓ | ✓ |
| North African amphorae | Arikamedu* Karur | | ✓* | ✓ | | ✓ | | ✓ |
| Torpedo jars | See Fig. 21 | | | | ✓ | | | ✓ |
| Mesopotamian Glazed Ware | ✓ | | | ✓ | ✓ | | ✓ | ✓ |
| LR Red Slip | | ✓ | ✓ | ✓ | | ✓ | ✓ | ✓ |

Table 3. Pottery types from Indian Ocean sites during the Late Roman period (*date uncertain).

*Sancti Arethae* of AD 524-5 (Wild & Wild 2001: 211), is significant and suggests that LR2 did not circulate in the Indian Ocean trade until after this date. The only Red Sea assemblage to include LR2 is from Adulis, where it is rare; unfortunately we do not know the situation for Clysma. At Elephanta in India, however, LR2 is common and provides tangible evidence for Mediterranean trade into at least the sixth century. Whether or how long it continued into the seventh century is an important question. Aqaba and other Late Roman amphora types were produced into the seventh century and possibly into the Early Islamic period, so both Adulis and Elephanta could easily extend into the seventh century, but their assemblages come from the surface and are difficult to date with precision.

Many amphora sherds in India previously thought to be Roman have been shown to be Mesopotamian Torpedo jars. There is strong evidence that some of these are of Sasanian date (Tomber 2007b), but others lack secure contexts and may be Early Islamic, as those from Sanjan certainly are (Nanji in preparation). Together with Mesopotamian Glazed Ware they are central in identifying the growing role of trade via the Gulf from at least the Sasanian period onwards.

Torpedoes occur primarily in North India and Sri Lanka, with South Indian examples from Pattanam and Alagankulam. They have not yet been identified along the Red Sea coast. Comparison of the Late Roman amphorae and Torpedoes in India and Sri Lanka is informative. Although they occur in the same region, they are only rarely found on the same site. Some may have travelled to India and Sri Lanka via Qana or Khor Rori, where they are present together (Sedov & Benvenuti 2002; Sedov 2007), but the overall pattern indicates two separate strands of trade: one from the Red Sea, the other via the Gulf. This is in keeping with what we know of the relations between Byzantium and the Sasanians, which were never simple. Procopius' sixth-century anecdote is oversimplified but demonstrates their economic rivalry, recounting Byzantium's failed attempt to gain control over the Sasanian-dominated silk trade by using the Aksumites as middlemen (*History of the Wars* 20.9-12). Archaeologically this antipathy is supported by evidence from northern Mesopotamia, where Simpson has shown that Sasanian and Roman finds respect political boundaries (Lang et al. 1998: 11). There were, however, select markets in the East where Roman and Sasanian goods were both available (Walburg 2008: 320-1) and they may provide yet another mechanism for the importation of Roman amphorae and Torpedo jars together into India during

167

the Late Roman or Early Islamic periods. As yet I have seen no finds to support this view.

Why, then, is there more visible unity around the Red Sea, both within and beyond the Roman world, during this period than earlier? The greater integration of Aila within this network first began with its annexation as a Roman province in AD 106, and for Aksum because of its international ascendancy. More important is the shared Christian culture that emanated from the Patriach of Alexandria. Apart from Hafun Main and the little known Marsa Nakari, all the active sites have a substantial Christian element represented structurally by churches, and in some cases artefacts, as described in the preceding chapters. Aila, Berenike, Aksum and Adulis were all thriving centres of Christianity, each the seat of a bishop, and together they form part of a Red Sea interaction zone (Tomber 2007a). Edessa was another important centre, and in the Tigris-Euphrates Valley and the borders of Persia there were over 20 bishoprics (Latourette 1954: 78-9), including one at Basra (Brown 1982: 66). Certainly Cosmas refers to a Persian church and clergymen in Sri Lanka (*Topography* 11.14).

Through trade came the movement of ideas and these shared ideas helped to solidify trading groups and partners. Just as Buddhism, for example, promoted trade in India from the Mauryan period by unifying merchants and trade sites, Christianity may have played a similar role in the West. Christianity is thought to have reached India through traders, from the Red Sea and from Mesopotamia via the Gulf. Despite the lack of archaeological evidence, India possesses a rich oral and textual tradition attributed to the Late Roman timeframe (Tomber 2007a). It should be remembered that Cosmas was himself both a trader and Christian theologian. Dark has suggested that Christianity promoted cultural unity some time in the sixth century, furthering economic cohesion and providing suitable conditions for the first phase of globalisation (2007: 14).

As we have discussed, Indian Ocean trade was a monumentally expensive business that reaped great profit. Christianity was an integrating force throughout the Indian Ocean, and the Church formed a powerful and wealthy institution. Therefore, one must consider whether the Church was a stakeholder in Eastern trade. It is commonly known that in the seventh century, the Church at Alexandria owned a large fleet. Shippers and traders, however, were primarily tied to the services of the Church for such duties as the distribution of grain during famine, with prohibitions against the direct involvement of clergy (Whittaker 1983: 168-9). Church agents were given tax dispensations for long distance trade *if* it was for charitable purposes, but a number of statutes in the fourth-century Theodosian code indicate that this privilege was frequently abused (ibid.: 169; *C.Th.* 13.1.16, 16.2.8, 16.2.10).

Through writings of the fifth- and sixth-century bishops, St Apollinaris and Gregory of Tours, Pieri has shown both the blurred distinction between some Eastern Mediterranean merchants and clergy, and the vast commercial wealth that merchants associated with the Church could accumulate (2002; 2005: 157-61). In his mid-third-century tract 'On those who fall', St Cyprian complained that even bishops 'chased after [foreign] markets of profitable business' (*De Lapsis* 6, trans. J.P. Wild; Ziethen & Klingenberg 2002: 382). Certainly, as recounted by the Byzantine monk John Moschus in the sixth century, an Alexandrian was loaned 50 pounds of gold by the Patriarch Apollinarius to cover shipping losses (Whittaker 2004: 170).

Indications of Church involvement in Eastern trade come mostly from oblique references (Tomber 2007a: 226). Ziethen and Klingenberg have shown that Christian fathers could be knowledgeable about items that circulated in Indian Ocean trade (2002: 380): in one case pearls and emeralds (Jerome

*Letters* 125.3-4). It has even been claimed that 'the patriarchate of Alexandria vigorously participated in the Red Sea maritime trade' (Letsios 1988: 350). An excerpt from the fourth-century *Liber Pontificalis* mentions that the Church at Rome received cinnamon, pepper, cloves and nard oil from estates, which they resold (Hopkins 1983: 87). It is clear that the Church was involved in Indian Ocean trade, but not necessarily in a regular or systematic manner. Christian sailors on trade ships were given the sacrament on the Red Sea coast before departing East (Tomber 2007a) and a graffito from Qana reminds us also of the input of Jewish merchants and sailors (Sedov 1997: 375-6).

Many Aqaba and LR1 amphorae have Christian monograms on them, including the chi-rho. Pieri has shown that Christian inscriptions on Mediterranean amphorae relate to ecclesiastical production and possibly also to where they were distributed (Pieri 2005: 175). Van Alfen, too, has demonstrated Church control over LR1 and its distribution (1996: 211-12). Similar arguments can be put forward for Aqaba amphorae and thus their distribution, clustering on sites facilitating Eastern trade, may underscore Church involvement or at the very least Christian merchants. Aqaba amphorae are bounded within Eritrea and generally non-coastal occurrences trace the route between Adulis and Aksum; this southern boundary seems to mark the limit of the Christian world.

Returning to the *Martyrium Sancti Arethae*, the Aksumite invasion of South Arabia is ostensibly interpreted as revenge for the persecution of Christians at Najran – an important pagan and later Christian pilgrimage centre located on the frankincense trade routes (Fig. 17; Doe 1971: 28). However, the main reason appears to be economic, ultimately relating to the power struggle between Byzantium and Persia (Hoyland 2003: 51; Ziethen & Klingenberg 2002: 383). Indeed, the *Martyrium* describes the warships as being manned by Roman, Ethiopian and Persian merchants (Glazier & Peacock 2007: 10).

## 6. Changing scenes and forces

### Transit and terminal

An assessment of the finds that travelled throughout the Indian Ocean reveals an active input from each region. The Romans played an important role in Indo-Roman trade during both the early and late periods, although some journeys were indirect and assisted by middlemen. Overall it is difficult to assess the absolute scale of trade. At present there is more archaeological evidence for the exchange of objects during the early period, but conversely the Red Sea sites intensify during the late period. Thus it is difficult even to assess the relative importance of each period.

Despite their obvious attraction, the large numbers of Roman coins in India do not resolve this question. There are growing numbers of late ones, which may eventually exceed the early issues in quantity although not value. Furthermore evaluating coinage on actual numbers will be misleading if the role of coinage differed through time or place. Increased recognition of Roman artefacts in India will play a role in future assessments of early versus late Indo-Roman trade. Already the recognition of Mesopotamian Torpedo jars has negatively impacted on the quantity of Roman sherds known from India, altered the distribution of Early Roman amphorae and increased what we know of trade via the Gulf.

The variable input of the different regions was largely determined by internal political and economic situations that impacted on their international relations (e.g. Salles 1998: 48). Thus, the changing fortunes of the Chera and Pandya kingdoms had a direct bearing on which ports Roman ships patronised (De Romanis 1997b: 90-108). Yet texts and even archaeology frequently provide only a snapshot of a single point in time. As a result, some of the most basic questions are difficult to answer, such as the relative importance of North and South India. Certainly their input altered through time

171

and they had a different range of products to offer. The very nature of an entrepot such as Muziris, in bringing together goods from throughout India, serves to mask archaeological patterns, as do indirect routes. Comparison of Roman coins between North and South India again fails, for contextual reasons. Nevertheless, in terms of the identification of artefacts, South India appears to have been more important to Egypt. The intensification of Western contact with Sri Lanka in the Late Roman period provides further compelling evidence, for South India played an active role in its expansion.

Entrepots such as Alexandria, Qana and Muziris were vital for amassing and redistributing goods. In the first instance, ships sailing from Berenike and Myos Hormos depended on what was available in Alexandria. Muziris, as we have seen, acted an entrepot for all of India, Qana was a redistribution node for East and West, and played a particularly important role for the Gulf.

What role the consumers, who would have been wealthy, played in the selection of specific items of import and export is difficult to assess, but consumer choice need not have been a determinant. It is hard to envisage a situation where specific types of wine, for example, had an Indian market, and easier to appreciate that wine as a generic class was desirable. While Romans resident in India may have had more specific demands, concentrations of individual amphora types in India could result merely from the single opportunistic trade deal of a merchant. In the West, was there a specific appetite for sapphires, for example, or were all gems valued equally?

Two levels of exchange may have existed at trading sites – one for locals and another for foreigners. In this context the clustering of imports at sites associated with trade and traders are important. At present, Indian pottery in Egypt is restricted to port sites and therefore appears to have been primarily for use there, or on board ships. None has yet been identified at

Alexandria. The potential exists for future finds, since we know through rare textual allusions that Indians stayed there. For example, in the second or third century, Xenophon of Ephesus mentioned an Indian rajah visiting Alexandria for sightseeing and trade (Xenophon 3.11.2; Casson 1989: 34).

Other Indian products, such as pepper and gems, are found both at the trade ports and elsewhere in the Empire and clearly functioned as items of both what Wheeler would have labelled terminal and transit trade. One would expect that Eastern goods intended for Western destinations would be recovered at transhipment points on the Red Sea, and this is indeed the case. Pepper was a transit item, but was also common at the Egyptian ports, partly identifiable due to preservation conditions. Cappers has suggested that its use at Berenike was viable because of the enormous quantities that were imported; in effect a surplus was created. Even travelling slightly away from the ports, into the Eastern Desert where similar preservation conditions exist, there is a drastic reduction in quantity (2006: 114, 165-6).

Alexandria provided a stepping off point for the rest of the Roman world. To date, Oriental finds are rarely published from elsewhere in the Empire – an Indian statuette from Pompeii is exceptional (During Caspers 1979). Investigation of durable items, such as stone and glass beads, is one means to explore archaeologically the penetration of this trade, particularly as source areas for glass become better understood through compositional analysis (Lankton & Dussubieux 2006). Indo-Pacific beads have been traced both to the West and East of their production centres at Arikamedu and Mantai (Francis 2004: 472-9). Beads are the only Indian/Sri Lankan find at Aksum and articulate that, together, the type of goods, the site and undoubtedly social circumstances determined whether trade was terminal or transit.

Indirect evidence is equally fruitful in tracing the geographical extent of this trade. From Britain there is good evidence for the importation of pepper. We know from an Early Roman writing tablet that pepper was available at Vindolanda on Hadrian's Wall (Bowman 1994: 70), while a silver shaker from Suffolk attests to its continued use during the Late Roman period (Johns forthcoming).

In this way it is possible to extend the debate beyond the fringe ports emphasised here into the heart of the Empire, and further to its most westerly shores. Nor were the effects of Indo-Roman trade restricted to this timeframe, but part of a continuum of far-reaching influence vividly seen in our dietary habits today, where pepper is considered a staple of life alongside salt.

# Endnotes

**1.** Amphora illustrations in Fig. 3 are from the following sources:

1. Knidian, after Grace 1949: pl. 19 no. 7.
2. Koan, after Martin-Kilcher 1994: Abb. 120, Nr. 10; Lawall 2003: fig. 108, no. 71.
3. Rhodian, after Hawkes & Hull 1947: pl. 71, no. 184.
4. Dressel 2-4, after Martin-Kilcher 1994: Abb. 120, Nr. 6.
5. Dressel 6A, after Scilliano & Sibella 1991.
6. Dressel 7-11, 38, after Panella 626, n. 11.
7. Dressel 20, after Scilliano & Sibella 1991.
8. Gauloise 4, after Laubenheimer 1985: fig. 134.
9. Amphore Egyptienne 3, after Ballet & Dixneuf 2004: fig. 13; Tomber 2006: fig. 1.55, no. 829.
10. Late Roman 1, after Van Alfen 1996: fig. 2.
11. Late Roman 2, after Böttger 1974: Abb 1, Bc.
12. Late Roman 3, after Egloff 1977: pl. 60, no. 2.
13. Late Roman 4, after Zemer 1977.
14. Late Roman 7, after Egloff 1977: pl. 59, no. 7.
15. Africana Grande, after Panella 1973: 629, n. 28.
16. Aqaba, after Whitcomb 1989: fig. 5a.
17. Torpedo, after Tomber 2007: fig. 4.

**2.** Main ceramic publication reference or source for amphora sites (RT = Roberta Tomber):

| Site no. | Site name | Ceramic publication | Examined by RT |
|---|---|---|---|
| 2 | Ajabpura | *IAR* 1968-9 | Yes |
| 3 | Akota | M.S. Baroda University | Yes |
| 4 | Alagankulam | Sridhar 2005 | Yes |
| 5 | Anuradhapura | Coningham & Batt 1999 | No |
| 6 | Arikamedu | Will 1996, 2004 | Yes |
| 10 | Bet Dwarka | Gaur et al. 2006 | No |
| 13 | Chaul | Gogte 2003 | Yes |
| 15 | Devnimori | Mehta & Chowdhary 1966 | Yes |
| 16 | Dwarka | Ansari & Mate 1966 | Yes |
| 17 | Elephanta | Gupta 2002; Tripathi 2004 | Yes |
| 18 | Hathab | Pramanik 2004 | Yes |
| 20 | Junnar | *IAR* 1957-8 | Yes |
| 21 | Kamrej | Tomber 2005a | Yes |
| 23 | Karaikadu | Raman 1992 | Yes |
| 25 | Karur | Tamil Nadu State Department of Archaeology | Yes |
| 27 | Kateshwar | K. Khandwalla | Yes |
| 29 | Kolhapur | Sankalia 1957 | No |
| 33 | Lothal | Tripathi 2004; Photo A. Tripathi | No |
| 35 | Maligamedu | Tamil Nadu State Department of Archaeology | Yes |
| 38 | Mantai | Coningham & Batt 1999; Carswell & Prickett 1984 | No |
| 39 | Mathura | Joshi & Sinha 1991 | No |
| 40 | Mylapore | St Thom Cathedral Museum, Chennai | Yes |
| 41 | Nagara | Mehta & Shah 1968 | Yes |
| 42 | Nani Rayan | M.S. Baroda University | Yes |
| 43 | Nasik | Deccan College Museum | Yes |
| 45 | Nevasa | Gupta et al. 2001 | Yes |
| 46 | Paithan | D. Kennet, pers. comm. | No |
| 49 | Pattanam | Shajan et al. 2008 | Yes |
| 50 | Paunar | Deo & Dhavalikar 1968 | Yes |
| 51 | Prabhas-Somnath | V. Shinde | Yes |
| 53 | Sanand | Gupta 1997 | Yes |
| 54 | Sanjan | Nanji in preparation | Yes |
| 58 | Taxila | Marshall 1975 | No |
| 62 | Tissamaharama | H. Schenk, H.-J. Weisshaar | Yes |
| 65 | Vallabipur | *IAR* 1957-8 | Yes |
| 66 | Vasavasamudram | Nagaswamy & Majeed 1978 | Yes |

# Bibliography

## Ancient sources

Antoninus Placentius, *Antonini Placentini Itinerarium*, ed. P. Geyer 1965 (*CCSL* 175) 127-53.

*CCSL* 175 = *Corpus Christianorum Series Latina 175: Iterinaria et Alia Geographica* (1965) (Turnhoult).

Claudius Ptolemy, *The Geography*, trans. and ed. E.L. Stevenson 1991 (1932 reprint) (New York: Dover Publications, Inc.).

Codex Theodosianus, *The Theodosian Code and Novels: and the Sirmondian Constitutions*, trans. and commentary C. Pharr 1952 (Princeton University Press).

Cosmas Indicopleustes, *Christian Topography*: see McCrindle 1897; Wolska-Conus 1968-73.

Cyprian, *De Lapsis*, in *Sancti Cypriani Episcopi Opera 1*, ed. M. Bévenot 1972 (*Corpus Christianorum Series Latina* 3, Turnhoult) 218-42.

Dio Cassis, *Dio's Roman History 8*, trans. E. Cary 1925 (Loeb Classical Library, London).

Dio Chrysostom, *Discourses 3: The Thirty-Fifth Discourse*, trans. J.W. Cohoon and H.L. Crosby 1951 (1940 reprint) (Loeb Classical Library, London) 389-415.

Egeria, *Itinerarium Egeriae*, ed. P. Geyer and O. Cuntz 1965 (*CCSL* 175) 35-103.

Jerome, *Select Letters of St Jerome*, trans. F.A. Wright 1938 (Loeb Classical Library, London).

Lucian, *Lucian 4, Alexander the False Prophet*, trans. A.M. Harmon 1925 (Loeb Classical Library, London) 174-253.

Pausaniaus, *Description of Greece 2: Laconia*, trans. W.H.S. Jones and H.A. Ormerod 1926 (Loeb Classical Library, London) 3-17.

*Periplus Maris Erythraei (PME)*, see Casson 1989.

Pliny the Elder, *Natural History 1, 2, 4*, trans. H. Rackham 1961-68 (reprint) (Loeb Classical Library, London).

177

Procopius, *History of the Wars 1*, trans. H.B. Dewing 1971 (1914 reprint) (Loeb Classical Library, London).

Quintus Curtius, *History of Alexander 2*, trans. J.C. Rolfe 1946 (Loeb Classical Library, London).

*Sangam* poetry: see Hart & Heifetz 1999; Zvelebil 1956.

Strabo, *Geography 2, 7, 8*, trans. H.L. Jones 1917-35 (Loeb Classical Library, London).

## Modern sources

Abraham, S. 2003 'Chera, Chola, Pandya: using archaeological evidence to identify the Tamil Kingdoms of Early Historic South India', *Asian Perspectives* 42(2): 207-23.

Abraham, S. 2005 'The Malabar Regional Archaeological Survey: introduction, goals, and prospects', *Journal of the Centre for Heritage Studies* 2: 1-5.

Abraham, S. 2007 'South Asian perspective', in Sidebotham & Wendrich 2007: 285-94.

Achaya, K.T. 1994 *Indian Food: A Historical Companion* (Delhi: Oxford University Press).

Achaya, K.T. 2002 (paperback 2nd reprint) *A Historical Dictionary of Indian Food* (New Delhi: Oxford University Press).

Albright, F.P. 1955 'Explorations in Dhofar, Oman', *Antiquity* 29: 37-9.

Albright, F.P. 1982 *The American Archaeological Expedition in Dhofar, Oman, 1952-1953* (American Foundation for the Study of Man 6, Washington DC).

al-Ansary, A.R. 1982 *Qaryat al-Fau: A Portrait of Pre-Islamic Civilisation in Saudi Arabia* (Al-Riyad: Jami'at al-Riya).

al-Kabawi, A., Khan, M., al-Mubarak, A., al-Tamai, M., al-Ubaid, S. and al-Subhan, I. 1989 'Preliminary report on the fourth season of comprehensive rock art and epigraphic survey of northern Saudi Arabia 1408 AH/1987 AD', *Atlal* 12: 41-51.

Amigues, S. 2005 (1996 trans. and reprint) 'A fantasmatic cinnamon', in Boussac & Salles 2005: 13-20.

Anfray, F. 1966 'La poterie de Matarā', *Rassegna di Studi Etiopici* 22: 5-74.

Anfray, F. 1974 'Deux villes d'Axoum: Adulis et Matarā', in *IV Congresso Internazionale de Studi Etiopici (Roma 10-15 Aprile 1972)* (Rome: Accademia Nazionale dei Lincei) 745-66.

Anfray, F. and Annequin, G. 1965 'Matarā: deuxième, troisième et quatrième campagnes de fouilles', *Annales d'Ethiopie* 6: 49-86.

178

# Bibliography

Ansari, Z.D. and Mate, M.S. 1966 *Excavations at Dwarka: 1963* (Deccan College Building Centenary and Silver Jubilee Series 44, Pune).

Audouin, R. 1991 'Sculptures et peintures du château royal de Shabwa', *Syria* 68: 165-81.

Avanzini, A. 2002 'The history of the Khor Rori area: new perspectives', in Avanzini 2002: 13-27.

Avanzini. A. (ed.) 2002 *Khor Rori Report 1* (Arabia Antica 1, Pisa).

Avanzini, A. and Orazi, R. 2001 'The construction phases of Khor Rori's monumental gate', *Arabian Archaeology and Epigraphy* 12: 249-59.

Avanzini, A. and Sedov, A.V. 2005 'The stratigraphy of Sumhuram: new evidence', *Proceedings of the Seminar for Arabian Studies* 35: 11-17.

Badré L. 1991 'Le sondage stratigraphique du Shabwa 1976-1981', *Syria* 68: 229-314.

Bagnall, R.S., Helms, C. and Verhoogt, A.M.F.W. 2000 *Documents from Berenike 1: Greek Ostraka from the 1996-1998 Seasons* (Papyrologica Bruxellensia 31, Brussels).

Bagnall, R.S. and Sheridan, J.A. 1994 'Greek and Latin documents from 'Abu Sha'ar, 1990-1991', *Journal of the American Research Center in Egypt* 31: 159-68.

Ball, W. 2001 (2000 paperback edn) *Rome in the East: The Transformation of an Empire* (London: Routledge).

Ballet, P. 1993 'Céramiques, faïences et vase en pierre du fonds Révoil', in Desanges et al. 1993: 63-72.

Ballet, P. 1996 'De la Méditerranée à l'océan Indien, l'Egypte et le commerce de longue distance à l'époque romaine: les données céramiques', *Topoi* 6(2): 809-40.

Ballet, P. and Dixneuf, D. 2004 'Ateliers d'amphores de la chôra Egyptienne aux époques romaine et byzantine', in Eiring & Lund 2004: 67-72.

Ballet, P. and Lemaître, S. forthcoming 'Le céramique importée', in J.P. Breton (ed.) *Fouilles de Shabwa 4* (Bibliothèque Archéologique et Historique, Beirut).

Bard, K.A., Fattovich, R., Manzo, A. and Perlingieri, C. 1997 'Archaeological investigations at Bieta Giyorgis (Aksum), Ethiopia: 1993-1995 field seasons', *Journal of Field Archaeology* 24: 387-403.

Begley, V. 1983 'Arikamedu reconsidered', *American Journal of Archaeology* 87: 461-81.

Begley, V. 1988 'Rouletted ware at Arikamedu: a new approach', *American Journal of Archaeology* 92: 427-40.

Begley, V. 1992 'Ceramic evidence for pre-*Periplus* trade on the Indian coasts', in Begley & De Puma 1992: 157-96.

Begley, V. 1996 'Changing Perceptions of Arikamedu', in Begley et al. 1996: 1-40.

Begley, V. 2004a 'Chronology', in Begley et al. 2004: 1-15.

Begley, V. 2004b 'Critique of V.D. Gogte's interpretations of X-ray diffraction analyses of Arikamedu pottery', in Begley et al. 2004: 631-42.

Begley, V. 2004c 'Pottery from the 1992 excavations in the southern sector', in Begley et al. 2004: 104-323.

Begley, V. and De Puma, R.D. (eds) 1992 (1991 reprint) *Rome and India: The Ancient Sea Trade* (Delhi: Oxford University Press).

Begley, V., Francis, P. Jr., Karashima, N., Raman, K.V., Sidebotham, S.E. and Will, E.L. 2004 *The Ancient Port of Arikamedu: New Excavations and Researches 1989-1992 2* (Ecole Française d'Extrême-Orient, Mémoires Archéologiques 22.2, Paris).

Begley, V., Francis, P. Jr., Mahadevan, I., Raman, K.V., Sidebotham, S.E., Slane, K.W. and Will, E.L. 1996 *The Ancient Port of Arikamedu: New Excavations and Researches 1989-92 1* (Ecole Française d'Extrême-Orient, Mémoires Archéologiques 22, Pondichéry).

Begley, V. and Sidebotham, S.E. 1996 'Field investigations 1989-92', in Begley et al. 1996: 41-66.

Begley, V. and Tomber, R. 1999 'Indian pottery sherds from Berenike', in Sidebotham & Wendrich 1999: 161-81.

Benoist, A., Mouton, M. and Schiettecatte, J. 2003 'The artefacts from the fort at Mleiha: distribution, origins, trade and dating', *Proceedings of the Seminar for Arabian Studies* 33: 59-76.

Berghaus, P. 1991 'Roman coins from India and their imitations', in Jha 1991: 108-21.

Bharucha-Irani, A. 2002 'Mandvi: an Early Historic sea port near the Gulf of Kachchh, Western India', *Man and Environment* 27(1): 69-72.

Bietak, M. and Schwartz, M. 1987 *Nag' el-Scheima, eine befestigte christliche Siedlung und andere christliche Denkmäler Sayala-Nubien 1. Die österreichischen Grabungen, 1963-1965* (Österreichischen Akademie der Wissenschaften, Philosophisch-Historische Klasse 191, Vienna).

Blue, L. 2006 'The sedimentary history of the harbour area', in Peacock & Blue 2006: 43-61.

# Bibliography

Boardman, S. and Gale, R. 2000 'Archaeobotanical methodology', in Phillipson 2000: 507-9 and *passim*.

Bonifay, M. and Leffy, R. 2002 'Les céramiques du remplissage de la cîterne du Sarapéion à Alexandrie', *Etudes Alexandrines* 6: 39-84.

Bopearachchi, O. 1997 'Forward', in Weerakkody 1997: ix-xxii.

Bopearachchi, O. 1998 'Seafaring in the Indian Ocean: archaeological evidence from Sri Lanka', in Ray & Salles 1998: 59-77.

Bopearachchi, O. 2006 'Coins', in Coningham 2006: 7-26.

Böttger, B. 1974 'Die Importkeramik aus dem spätantiken Donaulimeskastell Iatrus in Nordbulgarien', in D.M. Pippidi (ed.) *Actes du 9ᵉ Congrès International d'Etudes sur les Frontières Romaines. Mamaï, 6-13 septembre 1972* (Bucharest: Editura Academiei Republicii Socialiste România) 131-6.

Bourdon, C. 1925 *Anciens canaux, anciens sites et ports de Suez* (Cairo: Institute Français d'Archéologie Orientale).

Boussac, M.-F. and Salles, J.-F. (eds) 1995 *Athens, Aden, Arikamedu: Essays on the Interrelations between India, Arabia and the Eastern Mediterranean* (New Delhi: Manohar).

Boussac, M.-F. and Salles, J.-F. (eds) 2005 (some articles reprinted) *A Gateway from the Eastern Mediterranean to India: The Red Sea in Antiquity* (New Delhi: Manohar).

Bowen, R. LeBaron and Albright, F.B. 1958 *Archaeological Discoveries in South Arabia* (American Foundation for the Study of Man 2, Baltimore).

Bowman, A.K. 1994 *Life and Letters on the Roman Frontier: Vindolanda and its People* (London: British Museum Press).

Brancaccio, P. in press 'Moulding the West: moulds and the circulation of western models on the Deccan Plateau in the Sātavāhana period', Tomber et al. in press.

Brankaer, J. 2003 'Written material other than Latin or Greek', in Peacock et al. 2003: 45-6.

Breton, J.-F. 1989 'L'Orient gréco-romain et le Hadhramawt', in T. Fahd (ed.) *L'Arabie préislamique et son environnement historique et culturel, Actes du Colloque de Strasbourg, 24-27 juin 1987* (Travaux du Centre de Recherche sur le Proche-Orient et la Grèce Antiques 10, Leiden) 173-85.

Breton, J.-F. 2003 'Preliminary notes on the development of Shabwa', *Proceedings of the Seminar for Arabian Studies* 33: 199-213.

Brown, L. 1982 (2nd revised edn) *The Indian Christians of St Thomas: An Account of the Ancient Syrian Church of Malabar* (Cambridge University Press).

Bruyère, B. 1966 *Fouilles de Clysma-Qolzoum (Suez), 1930-1932* (Fouilles de l'Institute Français d'Archéologie Orientale 27, Cairo).

Bülow-Jacobsen, A., Cuvigny, H. and Fournet, J.L. 1994 'The identification of Myos Hormos: new papyrological evidence', *Bulletin de l'Institut Français d'Archéologie Orientale* 94: 27-38.

Burnett, A. 1998 'Roman coins from India and Sri Lanka', in O. Bopearacchi and D.P.M. Weerakkody (eds) *Origin, Evolution and Circulation of Foreign Coins in the Indian Ocean* (New Delhi: Manohar) 179-89.

Burstein, S.M. (trans. and ed.) 1989 *Agatharchides of Cnidus on the Erythraean Sea* (London: Hakluyt Society).

Burstein, S.M. 1996 'Ivory and Ptolemaic exploration of the Red Sea: the missing factor', *Topoi* 6(2): 799-807.

Calvet, Y. 1988 'Fouilles françaises de Shabwa (R.D.P. Yemen): la céramique importée', *Raydan* 5: 1-70.

Cappers, R.T.J. 2006 *Roman Foodprints at Berenike: Archaeobotanical Evidence of Subsistence and Trade in the Eastern Desert of Egypt* (Cotsen Institute of Archaeology Monograph 55, Los Angeles, University of California).

Carswell, J. 1990 'The excavation of Mantai', *Ancient Ceylon* 7: 17-28.

Carswell, J. and Prickett, M. 1984 'Mantai, 1980: a preliminary investigation', *Ancient Ceylon* 5: 3-80.

Casal, J.M. 1949 *Fouilles de Virampatnam-Arikamedu: rapport de l'Inde et de l'Occident aux environs de l'ère chrétienne* (Paris: C. Klincksieck).

Casal, J.M. and Casal, G. 1956 *Site urbain et sites funéraires des environs de Pondichéry: Virampatnam, Mouttrapaléon, Souttoukèny* (Publication de la Commission des Fouilles Archéologiques, Fouilles de l'Inde, Paris).

Casson, L. 1986 'P. Vindob G 40822 and the shipping of goods from India', *Bulletin of the American Society of Papyrologists* 23(3-4): 73-9.

Casson, L. 1989. *The Periplus Maris Erythraei: Text with Introduction, Translation and Commentary* (Princeton University Press).

Casson, L. 1995 'The Greek and Latin sources for the southwestern coast of Arabia', *Arabian Archaeology and Epigraphy* 6: 214-21.

Chakrabarti, D.K. 1999 *India: An Archaeological History. Palaeolithic Beginnings to Early Historic Foundations* (New Dehli: Oxford University Press).

Chakrabarti, D.K. 2004 (1995 digital reprint) 'Post-Mauryan states of mainland South Asia (c. BC 184-AD 320)', in F.R. Allchin, *The*

182

# Bibliography

*Archaeology of Early Historic South Asia: The Emergence of Cities and States* (Cambridge University Press) 274-326.

Chakravarti, R. 2002 *Traders and Trade in Early Indian Society* (Delhi: Manohar).

Chami, F.A. 1999 'Roman beads from the Rufiji Delta, Tanzania: first incontrovertible archaeological link with the *Periplus*', *Current Anthropology* 40: 237-41.

Chami, F.A. 2002 'People and contacts in the Western Indian Ocean seaboard of Azania', *Man and Environment* 27(1): 33-44.

Chami, F.A. 2004 'The Egypto-Graeco-Romans and Panchaea/Azania: sailing in the Erythraean Sea', in Lunde & Porter 2004: 93-103.

Champakalakshmi, R. 2006 (1996 reprint) *Trade, Ideology and Urbanization: South India, 330 BC to AD 1300* (New Delhi: Oxford University Press).

Chande, M.B. 1998 *Kautilyan Arthasastra* (New Delhi: Atlantic Publishers).

Chittick, N. 1974 'Excavations at Aksum, 1973-4: a preliminary report', *Azania* 9: 159-205.

Chittick, N. 1976 'An archaeological reconnaissance in the Horn: the British-Somali expedition, 1975', *Azania* 11: 117-33.

Chittick, N. 1979 'Early ports in the Horn of Africa', *International Journal of Nautical Archaeology* 8(4): 273-7.

Chowdhary, S.N. 1962 'A bronze statuette of Atlas from Śāmālājī', *Journal of the Oriental Institute, M. S. University of Baroda* 11(4): 309-15.

Comfort, H. 1958 'Imported pottery and glass from Timna' ', in Bowen & Albright 1958: 199-207.

Comfort, H. 1960 'Some imported pottery at Khor Rori (Dhofar)', *Bulletin of the American Schools of Oriental Research* 160: 15-20.

Comfort, H. 1992 'Terra sigillata at Arikamedu', in Begley & De Puma 1992: 134-50.

Coningham, R. 2006 *Anuradhapura: The British-Sri Lankan Excavations at Anuradhapura Salgaha Watta 2. 2: The Artefacts* (BAR Intl Ser. 1508, Oxford).

Coningham, R. and Batt, C. 1999 'Dating the sequence', in R. Coningham, *Anuradhapura: The British-Sri Lankan Excavations at Anuradhapura Salgaha Watta 2. 1: The Site* (BAR Intl Ser. 824, Oxford) 125-31.

Cooper, J.P. 2005 *The Nile-Red Sea Canal in Antiquity: A Consideration of the Evidence for its Existence, Duration and Route* (MA dissertation, University of Southampton).

Copeland, P. 2006 'Trench 2B', in Peacock & Blue 2006: 116-27.

Cribb, J. 2005 *The Indian Coinage Tradition: Origins, Continuity & Change* (Nashik: Indian Institute of Research in Numismatic Studies).

Curtis, I. 2001 *Ancient Food Technology* (Leiden: E.J. Brill).

Cuvigny, H. (ed.) 2003 *La route de Myos Hormos: l'armée dans le desert Oriental d'Egypte* (Fouilles de l'Institute Français d'Archéologie Orientale 48(1-2), Cairo).

Cuvigny, H. 2005 (1996 trans. and reprint) 'Researches in the Eastern Desert, 1996-1999', in Boussac & Salles 2005: 31-42.

Dalby, A. 2000 *Dangerous Tastes: The Story of Spices* (London: British Museum Press).

Dark, K.D. 2007 'Globalizing Late Antiquity: models, metaphors and the realities of long-distance trade and diplomacy', in A. Harris (ed.) *Incipient Globalization? Long-Distance Contacts in the Sixth Century* (BAR Intl Ser. 1644, Oxford) 3-14.

Das Gupta, P.C. 1960 'Graeco-Roman finds from Bengal', *Indo-Asian Culture* 8: 386-92.

Datoo, B.A. 1970 'Rhapta: the location and importance of East Africa's first port', *Azania* 5: 65-75.

Davidde, B. and Petriaggi, R. 1998 'Archaeological surveys in the harbour of ancient Kané', *Proceedings of the Seminar for Arabian Studies* 28: 39-44.

Davidde, B., Petriaggi, R. and Williams, D.F. 2004 'New data on the commercial trade of the harbour of Kanē through the typological and petrographic study of the pottery', *Proceedings of the Seminar for Arabian Studies* 34: 85-100.

*Dawn of Civilization in Maharashtra*, 1975 (Bombay: Prince of Wales Museum of Western India).

De Contenson, H. 1963 'Les fouilles à Axoum en 1958, rapport préliminaire', *Annales d'Ethiopie* 5: 1-40.

De Geest, P. 2006 'Caves and archaeology', in C. Cheung and L. DeVantier, *Socotra: A Natural History of the Islands and their People* (Hong Kong: Odyssey Publications) 19.

De Puma, R.D. 1992 'The Roman bronzes from Kolhapur', in Begley & De Puma 1992: 82-112.

De Romanis, F. 1996 *Cassia, cinnamomo, ossidiana: uomini e merci tra Oceano idiano e Mediterraneo* (Saggi di storia antica 9, Rome).

De Romanis, F. 1997a (1988 trans. and reprint) 'Romanukharaṭṭha and Taprobane: relations between Rome and Sri Lanka in the first century AD', in De Romanis & Tchernia 1997: 161-237.

# Bibliography

De Romanis, F. 1997b (1982-7 trans. and reprint) 'Rome and the *nótia* of India: relations between Rome and southern India from 30 BC to the Flavian period', in De Romanis & Tchernia 1997: 80-160.

De Romanis, F. and Tchernia, A. (eds) 1997 *Crossings: Early Mediterranean Contacts with India* (New Delhi: Manohar).

Dehejia, V. 1972 *Early Buddhist Rock Temples: A Chronological Study* (London: Thames and Hudson).

Deo, S.B. and Dhavalikar, M.K. 1968 *Paunar Excavation (1967)* (Nagpur University).

Desai, M.D. 1951 'Some Roman antiquities from Akota near Baroda', *Bulletin of the Baroda Museum and Picture Gallery 1949-50* 7: 21-3.

Desanges, J., Stern, M.E. and Ballet, P. 1993 *Sur les routes antiques de l'Azanie et de l'Inde: le fonds Révoil du Musée de l'Homme (Heïs et Damo, en Somalie)* (Mémoires de l'Académie des Inscriptions et Belles-lettres 13 nouvelle série, Paris).

Devasahayam, N. 1985 'Roman jewellery from Vellalore site during the Sangam period', *Lalit Kalā* 21: 53.

Dijkstra, M. and Verhoogt, A.M.F.W. 1999 'The Greek-Palmyrene inscription', in Sidebotham & Wendrich 1999: 208-18.

Dikshit, M.G. 1969 *History of Indian Glass* (Bombay: T.V. Chidambara).

Dilke, O.A.W. 1985 *Greek and Roman Maps* (London: Thames and Hudson).

Doe, B. 1971 *Southern Arabia* (London: Thames and Hudson).

Dolinka, B.J. 2003 *Nabataean Aila (Aqaba, Jordan) from a Ceramic Perspective* (BAR Intl Ser. 1116, Oxford).

Dressel, H. 1899 *Inscriptiones urbis Romae latinae: instrumentum domesticum* (Corpus Inscriptionum Latinarum 15(1), Berlin).

During Caspers, E.L.C. 1979 'The Indian ivory figurine from Pompeii – a reconsideration of its functional use', *South Asian Archaeology 1979*: 341-53.

Egloff, M., 1977. *Kellia: la poterie copte: quatre siècles d'artisanat et d'échanges en Basse-Egypte* (Recherches Suisses d'Archéologie Copte 3, Geneva).

Eiring, J. and Lund, J. (eds) 2004 *Transport Amphorae and Trade in the Eastern Mediterranean: Acts of the International Colloquium at the Danish Institute at Athens, September 26-29, 2002* (Monographs of the Danish Institute at Athens 5, Athens).

Elaigne, S. 1999 'Northern Black Polished Ware from Coptos', poster presented at the European Association of South Asian Archaeologists, Leiden 1999.

Elliot, W. 1844 'A discovery of Roman coins in the Coimbatore District', *Madras Journal of Literature and Science* 13(30): 211-15.

Fattovich, R. and Bard, K.A. 1993 'Scavi archeologici nella zona di Aksum. E. Ona Enda Aboi Zeugè e Ona Nagast (Bieta Giyorgis)', *Rassegna di Studi Etiopici* 37: 5-35.

Fattovich, R. and Bard, K.A. 1995 'Scavi archeologica nella zona di Aksum. G. Ona Enda Aboi Zeugè e Ona Nagast (Bieta Giyorgis)', *Rassegna di Studi Etiopici* 39: 50-80.

Finneran, N. 2007 *The Archaeology of Ethiopia* (London: Routledge).

Ford, L.A., Pollard, A.M., Coningham, R.A.E. and Stern, B. 2005 'A geochemical investigation of the origin of rouletted and other related South Asian fine wares', *Antiquity* 79: 909-20.

Foster, B.C., Rivard, J.-L.G., Sidebotham, S.E. and Cuvigny, H. 2007 'Survey of the emerald mines at Wadi Sikait 2000/2001 seasons', in Sidebotham & Wendrich 2007: 304-43.

Francis, P. Jr. 2000 'Human ornaments', in Sidebotham & Wendrich 2000: 211-25.

Francis, P. Jr. 2004 'Beads and selected small finds from the 1988-92 excavations', in Begley et al. 2004: 447-604.

Francis, P., Jr. 2007 'Personal adornments', in Sidebotham & Wendrich 2007: 251-7.

Freeman-Grenville, G.S.P., Chapman, R.L. III, and Taylor, J.E. 2003 *Palestine in the Fourth Century A.D.: The Onomasticon of Eusebius of Caesarea* (Jerusalem: Carta).

Friedmann, Y. (trans) 1992 *The History of al-Tabari 12: The Battle of al-Qadisiyah and the Conquest of Syria and Palestine* (Albany: State University of New York).

Fuks, A. 1951 'Notes on the archive of Nicanor', *Journal of Juristic Papyrology*: 207-16.

Gaur, A.S., Sundaresh and Tripati, S. 2006 'Evidence for Indo-Roman trade from Bet Dwarka waters, west coast of India', *International Journal of Nautical Archaeology* 35(1): 117-27.

Ghosh, A. (ed.) 1989 *An Encyclopaedia of Indian Archaeology 1: Subjects* (New Delhi: Munshiram Manoharlal).

Gibbon, E. with an Introduction by H. Trevor-Roper 1993 (1910 revised edn) *The Decline and Fall of the Roman Empire* (Everyman's Library 95, London).

Glazier, D. and Peacock, D. 2007 'The historical background and previous investigations', in Peacock & Blue 2007: 7-17.

# Bibliography

Gogte, V.D. 1997 'The Chandraketugarh-Tamluk region of Bengal: source of the Early Historic rouletted ware from India and Southeast Asia', *Man and Environment* 22(1): 69-85.

Gogte, V.D. 1999 'Petra, the *Periplus* and ancient Indo-Arabian maritime trade', *Annual of the Department of Antiquities of Jordan* 43: 299-304.

Gogte, V.D. 2001 'XRD analyses of the rouletted ware and other fine grey ware from Tissamaharama', in Weisshaar et al. 2001: 197-202.

Gogte, V.D. 2003 'Discovery of the ancient port of Chaul', *Man and Environment* 28(1): 67-74.

Goyon, J.-C. 2005 (1996 trans. and reprint) 'Remarks on F. De Romanis' book: the Egyptologist's point of view', in Boussac & Salles 2005: 7-11.

Grace. V. 1949 'Standard pottery containers of the ancient Greek world', *Hesperia Suppl.* 8: 175-89.

Gragg, G.B. 1979 'Himyaritic', in Whitcomb & Johnson 1979: 244-5.

Gragg, G.B. 1996 'South Arabian/Axumite dipinto', in Sidebotham & Wendrich 1996: 209-11.

Groom, N. 1981 *Frankincense and Myrrh: A Study of the Arabian Incense Trade* (London: Longman).

Groom, N. 1994 'Oman and the Emirates in Ptolemy's map', *Arabian Archaeology and Epigraphy* 5: 198-214.

Groom, N. 1995 'The *Periplus*, Pliny and Arabia', *Arabian Archaeology and Epigraphy* 6: 180-95.

Gupta, S. 1997 *Roman Egypt to Peninsular India: Archaeoloogical Patterns of Trade, 1st Century B.C.-3rd Century A.D.* (PhD thesis, Deccan College, Pune).

Gupta, S. 1998 'Nevasa: a type-site for the study of Indo-Roman trade in Western India', *South Asian Studies* 14: 87-102.

Gupta, S. 2002 'Amphora from Elephanta Island: a preliminary study', in Shinde et al. 2002: 79-81.

Gupta, S. 2007 'Frankincense in the "triangular" Indo-Arabian-Roman aromatics trade', in Peacock & Williams 2007: 112-21.

Gupta, S., Williams, D.F. and Peacock, D. 2001 'Dressel 2-4 amphorae and Roman trade with India: the evidence from Nevasa', *South Asian Studies* 17: 7-18.

Gurukkal, R. 1989 'Forms of production and forces of change in ancient Tamil society', *Studies in History* 5(2): 159-75.

Gurukkal, R. 1995 'The beginnings of the Historic Period: the Tamil South', in Thapar 1995: 237-65.

Gurukkal, R. and Whittaker, C.R. 2001 'In search of Muziris', *Journal of Roman Archaeology* 14: 335-50.

Haerinck, E. 1998a 'International contacts in the southern Persian Gulf in the late 1st century B.C./1st century A.D.: numismatic evidence from Ed-Dur (Emirate of Umm al-Qaiwain, U.A.E.)', *Iranica Antiqua* 33: 273-302.

Haerinck, E. 1998b 'The shifting pattern of overland and seaborne trade in SE-Arabia: foreign pre-Islamic coins from Mleiha (Emirate of Sharjah, U.A.E.)', *Akkadica* 106: 22-40.

Hahn, W. 1994-99 'Touto Arese Te Chora – St. Cyril's Holy Cross cult in Jerusalem and Aksumite coin typology', *Israel Numismatic Journal* 13: 103-17.

Hahn, W. 2000 'Aksumite numismatics: a critical survey of recent research', *Revue numismatique*: 281-311.

Hamilton-Dyer, S. 2001 'Faunal remains', in Peacock et al. 2001: 57-8.

Hamilton-Dyer, S. 2002 'Faunal remains', in Peacock et al. 2002: 67-71.

Handley, F.J.L. 2003 'The textiles', in Peacock et al. 2003: 57-60.

Harlow, M. 2000 'Glass and beads', in Phillipson 2000: 458-60 and *passim*.

Harrell, J.A. 1999 'Geology', in Sidebotham & Wendrich 1999: 107-21.

Hart, G.L. and Heifetz, H. (trans. and eds) 1999 *The Four Hundred Songs of War and Wisdom: An Anthology of Poems from Classical Tamil – The Puranānūru* (New York: Columbia University Press).

Hawkes, C.F.C. and Hull, M.R. 1947 *Camulodunum: First Report on the Excavations at Colchester 1930-1939* (Report of the Research Committee of the Society of Antiquaries of London 14, Oxford).

Hayes, J.W. 1996 'The pottery', in Sidebotham & Wendrich 1996: 147-78.

Hobbs, R 1995 'Roman coins from Merv, Turkmenistan', *Oxford Journal of Archaeology* 14(1): 97-102.

Hopkins, K. 1983 'Models, ships and staples', in P. Garnsey and C.R. Whittaker (eds) *Trade and Famine in Classical Antiquity* (Cambridge Philological Society Suppl. 8, Cambridge) 84-109.

Horton, M.C. 1996 'Early maritime trade and settlement along the coasts of eastern Africa', in Reade 1996: 439-59.

Hourani, G.F. 1995 (1951) revised and expanded by J. Carswell *Arab Seafaring in the Indian Ocean in Ancient and Early Medieval Times* (Princeton University Press).

Howell, J. and Sinha, A.K. 1994 'Preliminary report on the explorations around Sopara, Surat and Bharuch', *South Asian Studies* 10: 189-99.

# Bibliography

Hoyland, R.G. 2002 'Kings, kingdoms and chronology', in St. J. Simpson (ed.) *Queen of Sheba: Treasures from Ancient Yemen* (London: British Museum Press) 67-79.

Hoyland, R.G. 2003 (2001 reprint) *Arabia and the Arabs: From the Bronze Age to the Coming of Islam* (London: Routledge).

Huntingford, G.W.B. (trans. and ed.) 1980 *The Periplus of the Erythraean Sea by an unknown author; with some extracts from Agatharkhidēs 'On the Erythraean Sea',* (Hakluyt Society Second Series 151, London).

*IAR = Indian Archaeology, A Review.*

Ingraham, M.L., Johnson, T.D., Rihani, B. and Shatla, I. 1981 'Preliminary report on a reconnaissance survey of the northwest province', *Atlal* 5: 59-84.

Jahan, S.H. 2002 'Early maritime trade network of Bengal', *Man and Environment* 27(1): 127-38.

Jahan, S.H. 2005 'The role of the state in the maritime trade of Early Historic Bengal', *Man and Environment* 30(2): 74-82.

Jahan, S.H. 2006 *Excavating Waves and Winds of (Ex)change: A Study of Maritime Trade in Early Bengal* (BAR Intl Ser. 1533, Oxford).

Jasim, S.A. 1999 'The excavations of a camel cemetery at Mleiha, Sharjah, United Arab Emirates', *Arabian Archaeology and Epigraphy* 10: 69-101.

Jasim, S.A. 2006 'Trade centres and commercial routes in the Arabian Gulf: post-Hellenistic discoveries at Dibba, Sharjah, United Arab Emirates', *Arabian Archaeology and Epigraphy* 17: 214-37.

Jha, A.K. 1991 *Coinage, Trade and Economy. January 8th-11th, 1991. 3rd International Colloquium* (Nashik: Indian Institute of Research in Numismatic Studies).

Jha, A.K. and Rajgor, D. 1992 *Studies in the Coinage of the Western Ksatrapas* (Nashik: Indian Institute of Research in Numismatic Studies).

Johns, C.M. forthcoming *The Hoxne Late Roman Treasure: Gold Jewellery and Silver Plate* (London: British Museum Press).

Joshi, M.C. and Sinha, A.K. 1991 'Discovery of an amphora-handle from Mathura', in C. Margabundhu, K.S. Ramachandran, A.P. Sagar and D.K. Sinha (eds) *Indian Archaeological Heritage: Shri K.V. Soundara Rajan Festschrift* (Delhi: Agam Kala Prakashan) 255-9.

Jouveau-Dubriel, G. 1941 'Les ruines romaines de Pondichéry', *Bulletin de l'Ecole Fançaise d'Extrême-Orient, Hanoi* 40(2): 448-50.

Juma, A.M. 1996 'The Swahili and the Mediterranean worlds: pottery of the late Roman period from Zanzibar', *Antiquity* 70: 148-54.

189

Karttunen, K, 1989 *India in Early Greek Literature* (Studia Orientalia 65, Helsinki).

Keay, S.J. and Williams, D.F. 2005 *Amphora: A Digital Resource*, http://ads.ahds.ac.uk/catalogue/archive/amphora_ahrb_2005/ (Accessed April 2008).

Kennet, D. 2004 *Sasanian and Islamic Pottery from Ras al-Khaimah: Classification, Chronology, and Analysis of Trade in the Western Indian Ocean* (BAR Intl Ser. 1248, Oxford).

Kirwan, L.P. 1972 '*The Christian Topography* and the Kingdom of Axum', *Geographical Journal* 138: 166-77.

Kirwan, L.P. 1986 'Rhapta, metropolis of Azania', *Azania* 21: 99-104.

Kitchen, K.A. 2004 'The elusive land of Punt revised', in Lunde & Porter 2004: 25-31.

Kobishchanov, Y.M. 1979. *Axum* (University Park: Pennsylvania University Press).

Krishnamurthy, R. 2000 *Non-Roman Ancient Foreign Coins from Karur in India* (Chennai: Garnet Publishers).

Krishnamurthy, R. 2007 *Late Roman Copper Coins from South India: Karur, Madurai and Tirukkoilur* (Chennai: Garnet Publishers).

Lal Gupta, P. 1991 'Coins in Rome's Indian trade', in Jha 1991: 122-37.

Lang, J., Craddock, P.T. and Simpson, St. J. 1998 'New evidence for early crucible steel', *Journal of the Historical Metallurgy Society* 32: 7-14.

Lankton, J.W. and Dussubieux, L. 2006 'Early glass in Asian maritime trade: a review and an interpretation of compositional analyses', *Journal of Glass Studies* 48: 121-44.

Latourette, K.S. 1954 (2nd edn) *A History of Christianity* (London: Eyre and Spottiswoode).

Laubenheimer, F. 1985 *La production des amphores en Gaule Narbonnaise sous le haut-empire* (Centre de Rcherches d'Histoire Acienne 66, Paris).

Lawall, M. 2003 'Egyptian and imported transport amphoras', in S.C. Herbert and A. Berlin *Excavations at Coptos (Qift) in Upper Egypt, 1987-1992* (Journal of Roman Archaeology Suppl. 53, Portsmouth, RI) 157-91.

Lecomte, O. 1993 'Ed-Dur, les occupations des 3e et 4e s. ap. J.C.: contexte des trouvailles et matériel diagnostique', in U. Finkbeiner and R. Boucharlat (eds) *Materialien zur Archäologie der Seleukiden- und Partherzeit im südlichen Babylonien und im Golfgebiet: Ergebnisse der Symposien 1987 und 1989 in Blaubeuren* (Tübingen: E. Wasmuth) 195-217.

# Bibliography

Letsios, D.G. 1988 *Byzantium and the Red Sea: Relations with Nubia, Ethiopia and South Arabia until the Arab Conquest* (Historical Monographs 5, Athens).

Littmann, E. 1913 *Deutsche Aksum Expedition 1906* (Berlin: G. Reimer).

Lloyd, M. 1985 'The shipwreck at Iskandil Burnu', *International Nautical Association Newsletter* 12.3: 4-5.

Lowick, N.M. 1985 *Siraf 15. The Coins and Monumental Inscriptions* (London: British Institute of Persian Studies).

Lunde, P. and Porter, A. (eds) 2004 *Trade and Travel in the Red Sea Region:Proceedings of the Red Sea Project 1* (BAR Intl Ser. 1269, Oxford).

McCrindle, J.W. 1897 *The Christian Topography of Cosmas, an Egyptian Monk* (London: Hakluyt Society).

MacDowall, D.W. 1998 'The evidence of the gazetteer of Roman artefacts in India', in Ray & Salles 1998: 79-95.

McPherson, K. 1995 (2nd edn) *The Indian Ocean: A History of People and the Sea* (Delhi: Oxford University Press).

Mahadevan, I. 1996 'Tamil-Brāhmi graffito', in Sidebotham & Wendrich 1996: 206-8.

Mahadevan, I. 2007 'Tamil Brāhmi script in Egypt', *The Hindu*, 21 Nov 2007 http://www.hindu.com/2007/11/21/stories/2007112158412400. htm) (Accessed March 2008).

Majcherek, G. 2004 'Alexandria's long-distance trade in late Antiquity – the amphora evidence', in Eiring & Lund 2004: 229-37.

Mango, M.M. 1996 'Byzantine maritime trade with the East (4th-7th centuries)', *Aram* 8: 139-63.

Manzo, A. 2005 'Aksumite trade and the Red Sea exchange network: a view from Bieta Giyorgis (Aksum)', in Starkey 2005: 51-66.

Marshall, J.H. 1975 (1951 reprint) *Taxila: An Illustrated Account of Archaeological Excavations Carried out at Taxila under the Orders of the Government of India between the Years 1913 and 1934* (Delhi: Motilal Banarsidass).

Martin-Kilcher, S. 1994 *Die römischen Amphoren aus Augst und Kaiseraugst 2: Die Amphoren für Wein, Fishsauce, Südfrüchte (Gruppen 2-24) und Gesamtauswertung* (Forschunge in Augst 7/2, Augst).

Mattingly, H. 1932 'Coins from a site-find in British East Africa', *Numismatic Chronicle* 12: 175.

Mayerson, P. 1993 'A confusion of Indias: Asian India and African India in the Byzantine sources', *Journal of the American Oriental Society* 113(2): 169-74.

191

Mayerson, P. 1996 'Egeria and Peter the Deacon on the site of Clysma (Suez)', *Bulletin of the American Schools of Oriental Research* 33: 61-4.

Mehta, R.N. 1957 *Archaeology of the Baroda, Bharuch and Surat Districts up to 1300 AD* (PhD thesis, M.S. Baroda University).

Mehta, R.N. and Chowdhary, S.N. 1966 *Excavation at Devnimori: A Report on the Excavation Conducted from 1960 to 1963* (M.S. University Archaeology Series 8, Baroda).

Mehta, R.N. and Shah, D.R. 1968. *Excavations at Nagara* (M.S. University Archaeology Series 10, Baroda).

Melkawi, A., 'Amr, K. and Whitcomb, D.S. 1994 'The excavation of two seventh century pottery kilns at Aqaba', *Annual of the Department of Antiquities of Jordan* 38: 447-68.

Menon, A.S. 1970 (1967 reprint) *A Survey of Kerala History* (Kottayam: Sahitya Pravarthaka Co-operative Society).

Metzler, D. 1989 'Kaiserkult ausserhalb der Reichsgrenzen und römischer Fernhandel', in H.-J. Drexhage and J. Sünskes (eds) *Migratio et Commutatio* (St Katharinen: Scripta Mercaturae) 196-200.

Meyer, J.C. 2007 'Roman coins as a source for Roman trading activities in the Indian Ocean', in Seland 2007a: 59-67.

Miller, J.N. 1969 *The Spice Trade of the Roman Empire. 29 BC to AD 641* (Oxford: Clarendon Press).

Moreland, J. 2003 (2001 reprint) *Archaeology and Text* (London: Duckworth).

Morony, M.G. 1984 *Iraq after the Muslim Conquest* (Princeton University Press).

Morrison, H. M. 1989 'The glass', in Munro-Hay 1989c: 189-209.

Morrison, K.D. 2002. 'Introduction', in Morrison, K.D. and Junker, L.L. (eds) *Forager-Traders in South and Southeast Asia: Long-Term Histories* (Cambridge University Press) 21-40.

Mouton, M. 1992 *La peninsule d'Oman de la fin de l'âge du fer au début de la période sassanide (250 av.-350 ap. J.-C.)* (Thèse de Doctorat, Université de Paris, Pantheon-Sorbonne).

Mouton, M. 1999 'Mleiha: presentation du site et périodisation', in M. Mouton (ed.) *Mleiha 1. Environnement, stratégies de subsistence et artisanats* (Trauvaux de la Maison de l'Orient Méditerranéen 29, Lyon) 9-32.

Munro-Hay, S. 1982 'The foreign trade of the Aksumite port of Adulis', *Azania* 27: 107-25.

Munro-Hay, S. 1989a 'The al-Madhāriba hoard of gold Aksumite and late Roman coins', *Numismatic Chronicle* 149: 83-100.

# Bibliography

Munro-Hay, S. 1989b 'The British Museum excavations at Adulis, 1868', *Antiquaries Journal* 69: 43-52.

Munro-Hay, S. 1989c *Excavations at Aksum: An Account of Research at the Ancient Ethiopian Capital Directed in 1972-74 by the Late Dr Neville Chittick* (Memoirs of the British Institute in Eastern Africa 10, London).

Munro-Hay, S. 1991 *Aksum: An African Civilization of Late Antiquity* (Edinburgh University Press).

Nagaswamy, R. 1995 *Roman Karur: A Peep into Tamil's Past* (Madras: Brahad Prakashan).

Nagaswamy, R. and Majeed, A.A. 1978 *Vasavasamudram: A Report on the Excavation Conducted by the Tamil Nadu State Department of Archaeology* (Tamil Nadu Department of Archaeology Publication 50, Madras).

Nair, C.G. 2008 'Study points to 500 B.C. Kerala maritime activity', *The Hindu*, 9 January 2008, http://www.thehindu.com/2008/01/09/stories/2008010956451300.htm (Accessed May 2008).

Nanji, R. in preparation *The Study of Early Medieval Ceramics in India with Special Reference to Sanjan (Gujarat)* (PhD thesis, Deccan College, Pune).

Nath, A. 1995 'Antiquities of Graeco-Roman affinity from Adam, an inland mart of central India', *East and West* 45: 149-71.

Naumkin, V.V. and Sedov, A.V. 1995 'Monuments of Socotra', in Boussac & Salles 1995: 193-250.

Panella, C. 1973 'Appunti su un gruppo di anfore della prima, media e tarda età imperiale', in *Ostia 3: Le terme del Nuotatore: scavo dell'Ambiente V et di un Saggio nell'Area* (Studi Miscellanei 21, Rome) 460-633.

Papadopoulos, J.K. 1994 'A western Mediterranean amphora fragment from ed-Dur', *Arabian Archaeology and Epigraphy* 5: 276-9.

Paribeni, R. 1907 'Ricerche nel luogo dell'antica Adulis (Colonia Eritrea)', *Monumenti Antichi* 18: 439-572.

Parker, A.J. 1992 *Ancient Shipwrecks of the Mediterranean and the Roman Provinces* (BAR Intl Ser. 58, Oxford).

Parker, G. 2002 '*Ex Oriente Luxuria*: Indian commodities and Roman experience', *Journal of the Social and Economic History of the Orient* 45(1) 40-95.

Parker, G. 2008 *The Making of Roman India* (Cambridge University Press).

Parker, S.T. 1996 'The Roman 'Aqaba project: the 1994 campaign', *Annual of the Department of Antiquities of Jordan* 40: 231-57.

Parker, S.T. 1998 'The Roman 'Aqaba project: the 1996 campaign', *Annual of the Department of Antiquities of Jordan* 42: 375-94.

Parker, S.T. 2000 'The Roman 'Aqaba project: the 1997 and 1998 campaigns', *Annual of the Department of Antiquities of Jordan* 44: 373-94.

Parker, S.T. 2002 'The Roman 'Aqaba project: the 2000 campaign', *Annual of the Department of Antiquities of Jordan* 46: 409-28.

Parker, S.T. 2003 'The Roman 'Aqaba project: the 2002 campaign', *Annual of the Department of Antiquities of Jordan* 47: 321-33.

Peacock, D. 1993 'The site of Myos Hormos: a view from space', *Journal of Roman Archaeology* 6: 226-32.

Peacock, D. 2007a 'Pottery from the survey', in Peacock & Blue 2007: 79-108.

Peacock, D. 2007b 'Stone artefacts from the survey', in Peacock & Blue 2007: 109-24.

Peacock, D. and Blue, L. (eds) 2006 *Myos Hormos – Quseir al-Qadim: Roman and Islamic Ports on the Red Sea, Survey and Excavations 1999-2003* (Oxford: Oxbow).

Peacock, D. and Blue, L. (eds) 2007 *The Ancient Red Sea Port of Adulis, Eritrea: Results of the Eritro-British Expedition, 2004-5* (Oxford: Oxbow).

Peacock, D., Blue, L., Bradford, N. and Moser, S. 2000 *Myos Hormos – Quseir al-Qadim: A Roman and Islamic Port Site, Interim Report, 2000* (University of Southampton).

Peacock, D., Blue, L., Bradford, N. and Moser, S. 2001 *Myos Hormos – Quseir al-Qadim: A Roman and Islamic Port Site, Interim Report, 2001* (University of Southampton).

Peacock, D., Blue, L. and Moser, S. 2002 *Myos Hormos – Quseir al-Qadim: A Roman and Islamic Port Site, Interim Report, 2002* (University of Southampton).

Peacock, D., Blue, L. and Moser, S. 2003 *Myos Hormos – Quseir al-Qadim: A Roman and Islamic Port Site, Interim Report, 2003* (University of Southampton).

Peacock, D. and Williams, D.F. (eds) 2007 *Food for the Gods: New Light on the Ancient Incense Trade* (Oxford: Oxbow).

Peacock, D., Williams, D.F. and James, S. 2007 'Basalt as ships' ballast and the Roman incense trade', in Peacock & Williams 2007: 28-70.

Pedersen, R.K. 2000 'Under the Erythraean Sea: an ancient shipwreck in Eritrea', *International Journal of Nautical Archaeology Quarterly* 27.2/3: 3-13.

# Bibliography

Petech, L. 1950 *Northern India according to the Shui/Ching/Chu* (Rome: Istituto Italiano per il Medio ed Estremo Oriente).

Phillips, C., Villeneuve, F. and Facey, W. 2004 'A Latin inscription from South Arabia', *Proceedings of the Seminar for Arabian Studies* 34: 239-50.

Phillips, J. 2000 'Classical Aksumite pottery: surface treatment and decoration', in Phillipson 2000: 491-3 and *passim*.

Phillipson, D.W. 1998 *Ancient Ethiopia. Aksum: Its Antecedents and Successors* (London: British Museum Press).

Phillipson, D.W. 2000 *Archaeology at Aksum, Ethiopia, 1993-7. 1-2* (Memoirs of the British Institute in Eastern Africa 17, London).

Pieri, D. 2002 'Marchands orientaux dans l'économie occidentale de l'Antiquité tardive', in L. Rivet and M. Sciallano (eds) *Vivre, produire et échanger: reflets méditerranéens. Mélanges offerts à Bernard Liou* (Archéologie et Histoire Romaine 8, Montagnac) 123-32.

Pieri, D. 2005 *Le commerce du vin oriental à l'époque byzantine (V^e-VII^e siècles: le témoignage des amphores en Gaule* (Institute Français du Proche-Orient, Bibliothèque Archéologique et Historique 174, Beirut).

Potter, T.W. and Johns, C. 2002 *Roman Britain* (London: British Museum Press)

Potts, D.T. 1989 'The Danish excavation', *Mesopotamia* 24: 13-27.

Potts, D.T. 1990 *The Arabian Gulf in Antiquity 2: From Alexander the Great to the Coming of Islam* (Oxford: Clarendon Press).

Potts, D.T. and Cribb, J. 1995 'Sasanian and Arab-Sasanian coins from eastern Arabia', *Iranica Antiqua* 30: 123-39.

Pramanik, S. 2004 'Hathab: an Early Historic port on the Gulf of Khambhat', *Journal of Indian Ocean Archaeology* 1: 133-40.

Prickett-Fernando, M. 1990 'Durable goods: the archaeological evidence of Sri Lanka's role in the Indian ocean trade', in S. Bandaranayake, L. Dewaraja, R. Silva and K.D.G. Wimalaratne (eds) *Sri Lanka and the Silk Road of the Sea* (Colombo: Sri Lanka National Commission for UNESCO).

Priestman, S.M.N. 2005 *Settlement and Ceramics in Southern Iran: An Analysis of the Sasanian & Islamic Periods in the Williamson Collection* (MA dissertation, University of Durham).

Rajan, K. 1994 *Archaeology of Tamilnadu (Kongu Country)* (Delhi: Book Indian Publishing Co.).

Rajan, K. 1998 'Early maritime activities of the Tamils', in Ray & Salles 1998: 97-108.

Ramachandra, T.N. 1951 'Tāṁraliptī?' (Taṁluk)', *Artibus Asiae* 14: 226-39.

Raman, K.V. 1992 'Further evidence of Roman trade from coastal sites in Tamil Nadu', in Begley & De Puma 1992: 125-33.

Ramsay, J. 2006 'Comments on the imported plant remains from the Roman Aqaba Project', Paper presented at the American Schools of Oriental Research Meeting, 15-18 November, in 'The Economy of Aila, A Roman Port on the Red Sea' session organised by S.T. Parker.

Rao, S.R., Rao, T.C.S., Gaur, A.S., Tripathi, S., Sundaresh, Gudigar, P. 1995-6 'Underwater explorations off Poompuhar', *Journal of Marine Archaeology* 5-6: 7-17.

Raschke, M.G. 1975 'Archaeological evidence for Ptolemaic and Roman trade with India', *Proceedings of the XIV International Congress of Papyrologists, Oxford, 24-31 July 1974* (Greco-Roman Memoirs 61, London) 241-6.

Raschke, M.G. 1978 'New studies in Roman commerce with the East', *Aufstieg und Niedergang der Römischen Welt* 2 9.2: 604-1378.

Rathbone, D. 2001. 'The "Muziris" papyrus (SB XVIII 13167): financing Roman trade with India', in *Alexandrian Studies 2 in Honour of Mostafa el Abbadi,* Bulletin de la Société d'Archéologie d'Alexandrie 46: 39-50.

Ratnagar, S. 2006 (2004 reprint) *Trading Encounters: From the Euphrates to the Indus in the Bronze Age* (New Delhi: Oxford India Paperbacks).

Raunig, W. 2004 'Adulis to Aksum: charting the course of Antiquity's most important trade route in East Africa', in Lunde & Porter 2004: 87-91.

Ravitchandirane, P. 2007 'Stratigraphy and structural context at Arikamedu', *East and West* 57: 205-33.

Ray, H.P. 1985 'Trade in the western Deccan under the Sātavāhanas', *Studies in History* 1(1): 15-35.

Ray, H.P. 1991 'Trade in the Deccan under the Satavahanas: numismatic evidence', in Jha 1991: 58-61.

Ray. H.P. 1995a 'A resurvey of Roman contacts with the East', in Boussac & Salles 1995: 97-114.

Ray, H.P. 1995b 'Trade and contacts', in Thapar 1995: 142-75.

Ray, H.P. 1995c (1988 revised edn) 'The Yavana presence in ancient India', in Boussac & Salles 1995: 75-95.

Ray, H.P. 1996 'Early coastal trade in the Bay of Bengal', in Reade 1996: 351-64.

# Bibliography

Ray, H.P. 1998 (1994 reprint) *The Winds of Change: Buddhism and the Maritime Links of Early South Asia* (Delhi: Oxford India Paperbacks).

Ray, H.P. 2003 Review of *Symbols of Trade: Roman and Pseudo-Roman Objects Found in India*, http://eh.net/bookreviews/library/0937 (Accessed October 2007).

Ray. H.P. 2006 'The archaeology of Bengal: trading networks, cultural identities', *Journal of the Economic and Social History of the Orient* 49(1): 68-95.

Ray, H.P. and Salles, J.-F. (eds) 1998 (1996 reprint) *Tradition and Archaeology: Early Maritime Contacts in the Indian Ocean* (New Delhi: Manohar).

Reade, J. (ed.). 1996 *The Indian Ocean in Antiquity* (London: Kegan Paul International).

Reinach, A.J. 1912 'Rapport sur les fouilles de Koptos', *Bulletin de la Société Française des Fouilles Archéologiques* 1912: 81.

Ricci, C. and Fattovich, R. 1987 'Scavi archeologici nella Zona di Aksum. B. Bieta Giyorgis', *Rassegna di Studi Etiopici* 31: 123-95.

Rickman, G. 1971 *Roman Granaries and Store Buildings* (Cambridge University Press).

Robin, Chr. 1981 'Les inscriptions d'al-mi'sâl et la chronologie de l'Arabie méridionale au IIIe siècle de l'ère chrétienne', *Comptes rendus des séances, Academie des Inscriptions et Belles-lettres 1981*: 315-39.

Robin, Chr. 1984 'La civilization de l'Arabie méridionale avant l'Islam', in J. Chelhod (ed.) *L'Arabie du sud, histoire et civilization 1: Le people yéménite et ses racines* (Paris: G.-P. Maisonneuve et Larose) 195-224.

Rougé, J. 1988 'La navigation en mer Erythrée dans l'antiquité', in J.-F. Salles (ed.) *L'Arabie et ses mers bordières 1: Itineraires et voisinages. Séminaire de recherche 1985-1986* (Travaux de la Maison de l'Orient 16, Lyon) 59-74.

Rutten, K. 2007 'The Roman fine wares of ed-Dur (Umm al-Qaiwain, U.A.E.) and their distribution in the Persian Gulf and the Indian Ocean', *Arabian Archaeology and Epigraphy* 18: 8-24.

Salles, J.-F. 1993 'The *Periplus of the Erythraean Sea* and the Arab-Persian Gulf', *Topoi* 3(2): 493-523.

Salles, J.-F. 1998 'Antique maritime channels from the Mediterranean to the Indian Ocean', in C. Guillot, D. Lombard and R. Ptak (eds) *From the Mediterranean to the China Sea: Miscellaneous Notes* (Wiesbaden: Harrassowitz) 45-68.

Salles, J.-F. 2002 'Adaptation culturelle des céramiques hellénistiques? Importation et imitations de produits occidentaux en Inde', in F. Blondé, P. Ballet and J.-F. Salles (eds) *Céramiques hellénistiques et romaines: productions et diffusion en Méditerranée orientale (Chypre, Égypte et côte syro-palestinienne)* (Travaux de la Maison de l'Orient Méditerranéen 35, Lyon) 189-212.

Salles, J.F. 2005 (1996 trans. and reprint) 'Review of Himanshu P. Ray, *The Winds of Change: Buddhism and the Maritime Links of Early South Asia*', in Boussac & Salles 2005: 257-65.

Salomon, R. 1991 'Epigraphic remains of Indian traders in Egypt', *Journal of the American Oriental Society* 3(4): 731-6.

Salway, B. 2001 'Travel, *itineraria* and *tabellaria*', in C. Adams and R. Laurence (eds) *Travel and Geography in the Roman Empire* (London: Routledge) 22-66.

Sankalia, H.D. 1957 'Imported Mediterranean amphorae from Kolhapur', *Journal of the Royal Asiatic Society* 1957: 207-8.

Sankalia, H.D., Deo, S.B., Ansari, Z.D. and Erhardt, S. 1960 *From History to Pre-History at Nevasa (1954-56)* (Department of Archaeology and Ancient Indian History Deccan College Publication 1, Pune).

Sankalia, H.D. and Dikshit, M. 1952 *Excavations at Brahmapuri (Kolhapur) 1945-46* (Deccan College Monograph Series 5, Pune).

Saraswati, B. and Behura, N.K. 1966 *Pottery Techniques in Peasant India* (Memoir Anthropological Survey of India 13, Calcutta).

Sathyamurthy, T. 1992 *Catalogue of Roman Gold Coins* (Thiruvananthapuram: Department of Archaeology, Government of Kerala).

Schenk, H. 2001 'The development of pottery at Tissamaharama', in Weisshaar et al. 2001: 59-195.

Schenk, H. 2006 'The dating and historical value of rouletted ware', *Zeitschrift für Archäologie Außereuropäischer Kulturen* 1: 123-52.

Schenk, H. in press 'Parthian glazed pottery from Sri Lanka and the Indian Ocean trade' *Zeitschrift für Archäologie Außereuropäischer Kulturen* 2.

Schoff, W.H. (trans. and annotated) 1912 *The Periplus of the Erythraean Sea: Travel and Trade in the Indian Ocean by a Merchant of the First Century* (New York: Longmans, Green and Co.).

Sciallano, M. and Sibella, P. 1991 *Amphores, comment les identifier?* (Aix-en-Provence: Edisud).

Sedov, A.V. 1992 'New archaeological and epigraphical material from

Qana (South Arabia)', *Arabian Archaeology and Epigraphy* 3: 110-37.

Sedov, A.V. 1997 'Sea-trade of the Ḥaḍramawt kingdom from the 1st to the 6th centuries A.D.', in A. Avanzini (ed.) *Profumi d'Arabia, Atti de convegno 1997* (Rome: Bretschenider) 365-83.

Sedov, A.V. 1998 'Qana' (Yemen) and the Indian Ocean: the archaeological evidence', in Ray & Salles 1998: 11-35.

Sedov, A.V. 2007 'The port of Qana' and the incense trade', in Peacock & Williams 2007: 71-111.

Sedov, A.V. and 'Aydarus, U. 1995 'The coinage of ancient Hadramawt: the Pre-Islamic coins in the al-Mukallâ Museum', *Arabian Archaeology and Epigraphy* 6: 15-60.

Sedov A.V. and Benvenuti, C. 2002 'The pottery of Sumhuram: general typology', in Avanzini 2002: 177-248.

Seeger, J.A. 2001 'A preliminary report on the 1999 field season at Marsa Nakari', *Journal of the American Research Center in Egypt* 38: 77-88.

Seely, P., Canby, S. and Coningham, R. 2006 'Glazed ceramics', in Coningham 2006: 99-107.

Segall, B. 1958 'The lion-riders from Timna'', in Bowen & Albright 1958: 155-78.

Seland, E.H. 2006 *Indian Ocean in Antiquity: Trade and the Emerging State* (PhD thesis, University of Bergen).

Seland E.H. (ed.) 2007a *The Indian Ocean in the Ancient Period: Definite Places, Translocal Exchange* (BAR Intl Ser. 1593, Oxford).

Seland, E.H. 2007b 'Ports, Ptolemy, *Periplus* and Poetry – Romans in Tamil South India and on the Bay of Bengal', in Seland 2007a: 69-82.

Selvakumar, V. 2004 'Impressed pottery from the 1990-92 excavations', in Begley et al. 2004: 613-21.

Selvakumar, V. and Darsana, S. 2008 'Genesis and development of urban processes in the ancient/Early Historic Tamil Country', in G. Sengupta and S. Chakrabarti (eds) *Archaeology of Early Historic South Asia* (Kolkata: Pragati Publication) 337-72.

Selvakumar, V., Gopi, P.K. and Shajan, K.P. 2005 'Trial excavations at Pattanam, Paravur Taluk, Ernakulam District, Kerala – a preliminary report', *Journal of the Centre for Heritage Studies* 2: 57-66.

Selvakumar, V., Shajan, K.P. and Tomber, R. in press 'Archaeological investigations at Pattanam, Kerala, India: new evidence for the location of ancient Muziris', in Tomber et al. in press.

Sengupta, G. 1998 'Archaeology of coastal Bengal', in Ray & Salles 1998: 115-28.

Shajan, K.P. 1998 *Studies on Late Quaternary Sediments and Sea Level Changes of the Central Kerala Coast, India* (PhD thesis, Cochin University of Science and Technology).

Shajan, K.P., Cherian, P.J., Tomber, R. and Selvakumar, V. 2008 'The external connections of Early Historic Pattanam, India: the ceramic evidence', *Antiquity* 82, On-line Project Gallery.

Shajan, K.P., Tomber, R., Selvakumar, V. and Cherian, P.J. 2004 'Locating the ancient port of Muziris: fresh findings from Pattanam', *Journal of Roman Archaeology* 17: 351-9.

Sharma, P.C., Yelne, M.B. and Dennis, T.J. 2002 *Database on Medicinal Plants Used in Ayurveda 5* (New Delhi: Central Council for Research in Ayurveda & Siddha).

Shastri, S.M. 2000 'Introduction', in J.W. McCrindle (1927 revised edn) *Ancient India as Described by Ptolemy* (New Delhi: Munshiram Manoharlal) xiii-xxvii.

Shinde, V., Gupta, S. and Rajgor, D. 2002 'An archaeological reconnaissance of the Konkan coast: from Bharuch to Janjira', *Man and Environment* 27(1): 73-82.

Sidebotham, S.E. 1986 *Roman Economic Policy in the Erythra Thalassa 30 B.C.-A.D. 217* (Leiden: E.J. Brill).

Sidebotham, S.E. 1992 'Ports of the Red Sea and the Arabia-India trade', in Begley & De Puma: 12-38.

Sidebotham, S.E. 1994 'Preliminary report on the 1990-1991 seasons of fieldwork at 'Abu Sha'ar (Red Sea coast)', *Journal of the American Research Center in Egypt* 31: 133-58.

Sidebotham, S.E. 1996a 'The chariot seal impression', in Begley et al. 1996: 389.

Sidebotham, S.E. 1996b 'Roman interests in the Red Sea and Indian Ocean', in Reade 1996: 287-308.

Sidebotham, S.E. 2002 'Late Roman Berenike', *Journal of the American Research Center in Egypt* 39: 217-40.

Sidebotham, S.E. 2004 'Reflections of ethnicity in the Red Sea commerce in Antiquity: evidence of trade goods, languages and religions from the excavations at Berenike', in Lunde & Porter 2004: 105-15.

Sidebotham, S.E. 2007 'Coins', in Sidebotham & Wendrich 2007: 200-10.

Sidebotham, S.E. and Wendrich, W.Z. (eds) 1995 *Berenike 1994: Preliminary Report of the Excavations at Berenike (Egyptian Red*

*Sea Coast) and the Survey of the Eastern Desert* (Leiden: Centre for Non-Western Study).

Sidebotham, S.E. and Wendrich, W.Z. (eds) 1996 *Berenike 1995: Preliminary Report of the Excavations at Berenike (Egyptian Red Sea Coast) and the Survey of the Eastern Desert* (Leiden: Centre for Non-Western Study).

Sidebotham, S.E. and Wendrich, W.Z. (eds) 1998 *Berenike 1996: Report of the Excavations at Berenike (Egyptian Red Sea Coast) and the Survey of the Eastern Desert* (Leiden: Centre for Non-Western Study).

Sidebotham, S.E. and Wendrich, W.Z. (eds) 1999 *Berenike 1997: Report of the 1997 Excavations at Berenike and the Survey of the Egyptian Eastern Desert, including Excavations at Shenshef* (Leiden: Centre for Non-Western Study).

Sidebotham, S.E. and Wendrich, W.Z. (eds) 2000 *Berenike 1998: Report of the 1998 Excavations at Berenike and the Survey of the Egyptian Eastern Desert, including Excavations in Wadi Kalalat* (Leiden: Centre for Non-Western Study).

Sidebotham, S.E. and Wendrich, W.Z. 2001-2 'Berenike: archaeological fieldwork at a Ptolemaic-Roman port on the Red Sea coast of Egypt 1999-2001', *Sahara* 13: 23-50.

Sidebotham, S.E. and Wendrich, W.Z. (eds) 2007. *Berenike 1999/2000: Report on the Excavations at Berenike, including Excavations in Wadi Kalalat and Siket, and the Survey of the Mons Smaragdus Region* (University of California, Los Angeles: Cotsen Institute of Archaeology).

Sidebotham, S.E., Zitterkopf, R.E. and Tomber, R. in preparation 'Survey of the Via Hadriana: final report'.

Silva, R. 1985 'Mantai – a second Arikamedu?', *Antiquity* 59: 46-7.

Simpson, St. J. 2003 'From Mesopotamia to Merv: reconstructing patterns of consumption in Sasanian households', in T. Potts, M. Roaf, and D. Stein (eds) *Culture Through Objects: Ancient Near Eastern Studies in Honour of P.R.S. Moorey* (Oxford: Griffith Institute) 347-75.

Sinclair, P.J.J. 2007 'What is the archaeological evidence for external trading contacts on the East African coast in the first millennium BC?', in Starkey et al. 2007: 187-94.

Singer, C. 2007 'The incense kingdoms of Yemen: an outline history of the South Arabian incense trade', in Peacock & Williams 2007: 4-27.

Singh, A.K. 1977-8 'Pottery and trade – a study of Roman pottery from Indian sites', *Journal of the Bihar Research Society* 63(4): 140-74.

Slane, K.W. 1992 'Observations on Mediterranean amphoras and table-wares found in India', in Begley & De Puma 1992: 204-15.

Slane, K.W. 1996 'Other ancient ceramics imported from the Mediterranean', in Begley et al. 1996: 351-68.

Smith, M. 2002 'The role of local trade networks in the Indian subcontinent during the Early Historic period', *Man and Environment* 27(1): 139-51.

Smith, M.C. and Wright, H.T. 1988 'The ceramics from Ras Hafun in Somalia: notes on a classical maritime site', *Azania* 23: 115-41.

Sridhar, T.S. (ed.) 2005 *Alagankulam: An Ancient Roman Port City of Tamil Nadu* (Chennai: Department of Archaeology Government of Tamilnadu).

Starkey, J.C.M. (ed.) 2005 *People of the Red Sea: Proceedings of the Red Sea Project 2* (BAR Intl Ser. 1395, Oxford).

Starkey, J.C.M., Starkey, P. and Wilkinson, T. (eds) 2007 *Natural Resources and Cultural Connections of the Red Sea: Proceedings of the Red Sea Project 3* (BAR Intl Ser. 1661, Oxford).

Stern, B., Connan, J., Blakelock, E., Jackman, R., Coningham, R.A.E. and Heron, C. 2008 'From Susa to Anuradhapura: reconstructing aspects of trade and exchange in bitumen-coated ceramic vessels between Iran and Sri Lanka from the third to the ninth centuries AD', *Archaeometry* 50: 409-28.

Stern, E.M. 1993 'The glass from Heis', in Desanges et al. 1993: 21-61.

Stucky, R. 1983 'Ein Reise nach Marib, in die Stadt der Königin von Saba', *Antike Welt* 14(1): 2-13.

Subbarao, B. 1956 *The Personality of India: A Study in the Development of Material Culture of India and Pakistan* (M.S. University Archaeology Series 3, Baroda).

Sundström, R. 1907 'Report on an expedition to Adulis', *Zeitschrift für Assyriologie* 20: 171-92.

Suresh, S. 2004 *Symbols of Trade: Roman and Pseudo-Roman Objects Found in India* (New Delhi: Manohar).

Tchernia, A. 1997a (1992 trans. and reprint) 'The dromedary of the *Peticii* and trade with the East', in De Romanis & Tchernia 1997: 238-49.

Tchernia, A. 1997b (1995 trans. and reprint) 'Winds and coins: from the supposed discovery of the monsoon to the *denarii* of Tiberius', in De Romanis & Tchernia 1997: 250-76.

Thapar, R. (ed.) 1995 *Recent Perspectives of Early Indian History* (Bombay: Popular Prakashan).

Thapar, R. 1997 'Early Mediterranean contacts with India: an overview', in De Romanis & Tchernia 1997: 11-40.

Thapar, R. 2002 *The Penguin History of Early India: From the Origins to AD 1300* (London: Penguin Books).

Thomas, R. 2007 'The *Arabaegypti Ichthyophagi*: cultural connections with Egypt and the maintenance of identity', in Starkey et al. 2007: 149-60.

Thomas, R. and Masser, P. 2006 'Trench 8', in Peacock & Blue 2006: 127-40.

Thomas, R., Niemi, T.M. and Parker, S.T. 2007 'Structural damage from earthquakes in the second-ninth century at the archaeological site of Aila in Aqaba, Jordan', *Bulletin of the American Schools of Oriental Research* 346: 59-77.

Tomber, R. 2000 'Indo-Roman trade: the ceramic evidence from Egypt', *Antiquity* 74: 624-31.

Tomber, R. 2004a 'Amphorae from the Red Sea and their contribution to the interpretation of late Roman trade beyond the Empire', in Eiring & Lund 2004: 393-402.

Tomber, R. 2004b 'Rome and South Arabia: new artefactual evidence from the Red Sea', *Proceedings of the Seminar for Arabian Studies* 34: 351-60.

Tomber, R. 2005a 'Aksumite and other imported pottery from Kamrej, Gujarat', *Journal of Indian Ocean Archaeology* 2: 99-102.

Tomber, R. 2005b 'Troglodites and trogodites: exploring interaction on the Red Sea during the Roman period' , in Starkey 2005: 41-9.

Tomber, R. 2006 'The pottery', in V.A. Maxfield and D. Peacock (eds) *Survey and Excavations, Mons Claudianus 1987-1993. 3: Ceramic Vessels and Related Objects from Mons Claudianus* (Fouilles de l'Institute Français d'Archéologie Orientale 54, Cairo) 1-236.

Tomber, R. 2007a 'Bishops and traders: the role of Christianity in the Indian Ocean during the Roman period', in Starkey et al. 2007: 219-28.

Tomber, R. 2007b 'Rome and Mesopotamia – importers into India in the first millennium AD', *Antiquity* 81: 972-88.

Tomber, R. and Begley, V. 2000 'Indian pottery sherds', in Sidebotham & Wendrich 2000: 149-67.

Tomber, R., Blue, L. and Abraham, S. (eds) in press *Issues in Indian Ocean Commerce and the Archaeology of Western India* (European

Association for South Asian Archaeologists Bi-Annual Conference, London 2005).

Tomber, R., Cartwright, C. and Gupta, S. in preparation 'Rice tempered pottery from India'.

Tripathi, A. 2004 'Onshore and offshore exploration in Elephanta Island: evidence of Indo-Mediterranean trade', *Journal of Indian Ocean Archaeology* 1: 116-23.

Tripathi, S. 2002 'Early maritime activities of Orissa, east coast of India: linkages in trade and cultural developments', *Man and Environment* 27(1): 117-26.

Turner, P.J. 1989 *Roman Coins from India* (Institute of Archaeology Occasional Publication 12, London).

Turner, P.J. and Cribb, J. 1996 'Numismatic evidence for the Roman trade with ancient India', in Reade 1996: 309-19.

Van Alfen, P.G. 1996 'New light on the 7th-century Yassi Ada ship-wreck: capacities and standard sizes of LRA1 amphoras', *Journal of Roman Archaeology* 9: 188-213.

Van der Veen, M. 2001 'The plant remains: diet and fuel in Roman Myos Hormos', in Peacock et al. 2001: 59-61.

Van der Veen, M. 2004 'The merchants' diet: food remains from Roman and medieval Quseir al-Qadim', in Lunde & Porter 2004: 123-30.

Van Neer, W. and Ervynck, A.M.H. 1999 'The faunal remains', in Sidebotham & Wendrich 1999: 325-48.

Van Rengen, W. 2000 'The written material', in Peacock et al. 2000: 51-2.

Van Rengen, W. 2002 'Sebakh excavations and the written material', in Peacock et al. 2002: 53-4.

Van Rengen, W. 2003 'The written material', in Peacock et al. 2003: 43-5.

Verhoogt, A.M.F.W. 1998 'Greek and Latin texts', in Sidebotham & Wendrich 1998: 193-8.

Vermeeren, C.E. 1999 'Wood and charcoal', in Sidebotham & Wendrich 1999: 307-24.

Vermeeren, C.E. 2000 'Wood and charcoal', in Sidebotham & Wendrich. 2000: 311-42.

Vogel, J. 1952 'Notes on Ptolemy', *Bulletin of the School of African and Oriental Studies* 14: 78-86.

Walburg, R. 2001 'The coins from Tissamaharama, Godavaya and Ambalantota (1995-1998): an annotated catalogue', in Weisshaar et al. 2001: 261-74.

Walburg, R. 2008 *Coins and Tokens from Ancient Ceylon* (Forschungen zur Archäologie Außereuropäischer Kulturen 5, Wiesbaden).

Ward, W. 2002 *Roman Red Sea Ports: Berenike, Myos Hormos, Clysma,*

# Bibliography

*Leuke Kome, and Aila from Augustus to Diocletian* (MA dissertation, North Carolina State University, Raleigh).

Ward, W. 2007 'Aila and Clysma: the rise of northern ports in the Red Sea in late Antiquity', in Starkey et al. 2007: 161-71.

Warmington, E.H. 1928 *The Commerce between the Roman Empire and India* (Cambridge University Press).

Weerakkody, D.P.M. 1997 *Taprobanê: Ancient Sri Lanka as known to Greeks and Romans* (Indicopleustoi Archaeologies of the Indian Ocean 1, Turnhout).

Weisshaar, H.-J., Roth, H. and Wijeyapala, W. 2001 *Ancient Ruhuna: Sri Lankan-German Archaeological Project in the Southern Province. 1* (Materialien zur Allgemeinen und Vergleichenden Archäologie Band 58, Mainz am Rhein).

Wellstead, J.R. 1838 (reprint Graz 1978) *Travels in Arabia 2* (London: John Murray).

Wendrich, W.Z. 2007 'Basketry and matting', in Sidebotham & Wendrich 2007: 228-50.

Wendrich, W.Z., Tomber, R., Sidebotham, S.E., Harrell, J.A., Cappers, R.T.S. and Bagnall, R.S. 2003 'Berenike crossroads: the integration of information', *Journal of the Social and Economic History of the Orient* 46(1): 46-87.

Wheeler, R.E.M. 1951 'Roman contact with India, Pakistan and Afghanistan', in W.F. Grimes (ed.) *Aspects of Archaeology in Britain and Beyond: Essays Presented to O.G.S. Crawford* (London: H.W. Edwards) 345-81.

Wheeler, R.E.M. 1954a *Archaeology from the Earth* (Oxford: Clarendon Press).

Wheeler, R.E.M. 1954b *Rome Beyond the Imperial Frontiers* (London: Bell).

Wheeler, R.E.M. 1955 (3rd edn) *Still Digging: Interleaves from an Antiquary's Notebook* (London: Michael Joseph).

Wheeler, R.E.M. 1976 *My Archaeological Mission to India and Pakistan* (London: Thames and Hudson).

Wheeler, R.E.M., Ghosh, A. and Krishna Deva 1946 'Arikamedu: an Indo-Roman trading station on the east coast of India', *Ancient India* 2: 17-124.

Whitbread, I.K. 1995 *Greek Transport Amphorae: A Petrological and Archaeological Study*, (British School at Athens Fitch Laboratory Occasional Paper 4, Athens).

Whitcomb, D.S. 1982 'Roman ceramics', in Whitcomb & Johnson 1982: 51-115.

Whitcomb, D.S. 1989 'Evidence of the Umayyad period from the Aqaba excavations', in M.A. Bakhit and R. Shick (eds) *The Fourth International Conference on the History of Bilad al-Sham during the Umayyad Period* (Amman: al-Jāmi'ah al-Urdunīyah, Jāmi'at al-Yamūk) 164-8.

Whitcomb, D.S. 1994 *Ayla: Art and Industry in the Islamic Port of Aqaba* (Chicago: Oriental Institute).

Whitcomb, D.S. 1996 'Quseir al-Qadim and the location of Myos Hormos', *Topoi* 6(2): 747-72.

Whitcomb D.S. and Johnson, J.H. 1979 *Quseir al-Qadim 1978: Preliminary Report* (American Research Center in Egypt Reports 1, Cairo).

Whitcomb D.S. and Johnson, J.H. 1982 *Quseir al-Qadim 1980: Preliminary Report* (American Research Center in Egypt Reports 7, Malibu).

Whitehouse, D. 1989 'Begram, the *Periplus* and Gandharan art', *Journal of Roman Archaeology* 2: 93-100.

Whitehouse, D. 1990 'Review of the *Periplus Maris Erythraei*', *Journal of Roman Archaeology* 3: 489-93.

Whitehouse, D. 1998 *Excavations at ed-Dur (Umm al-Qaiwain, United Arab Emirates) 1: The Glass Vessels* (Leuven: Peeters).

Whitehouse, D. 2000 'Ancient glass from ed-Dur (Umm al-Qaiwain, U.A.E.) 2. Glass excavated by the Danish expedition', *Arabian Archaeology and Epigraphy* 11: 87-128.

Whitehouse, D. and Williamson, A. 1973 'Sasanian maritime trade', *Iran* 11: 29-49.

Whitewright, J. 2007a 'How fast is fast? Technology, trade and speed under sail in the Roman Red Sea', in Starkey et al. 2007: 77-87.

Whitewright, J. 2007b 'Roman rigging material from the Red Sea port of Myos Hormos', *International Journal of Nautical Archaeology* 36: 282-92.

Whittaker, C.R. 1983 'Late Roman trade and traders', in P. Garnsey, K. Hopkins and C.R. Whittaker (eds) *Trade in the Ancient Economy* (London: Chatto & Windus) 163-80.

Whittaker, C.R. 1998. ' "To reach out to India and pursue the dawn": the Roman view of India', *Studies in History* 14(1): 1-20.

Whittaker, C.R. 2004 (2000 trans. and reprint) 'Indian trade within the Roman imperial network', in *Rome and its Frontiers: The Dynamics of Empire* (London: Routledge) 163-80.

Wild, J.P. and Wild, F. 2000 'Textiles', in Sidebotham & Wendrich 2000: 251-74.

# Bibliography

Wild, J. P. and Wild, F. 2001 'Sails from the Roman port at Berenike, Egypt', *International Journal of Nautical Archaeology* 30: 211-20.

Wild, J.P. and Wild, F. 2007 'Textiles', in Sidebotham & Wendrich 2007: 225-7.

Wilkinson, J. 1981 (1971 revised edn) *Egeria's Travels to the Holy Land* (Warminster: Aris & Phillips).

Will, E.L. 1992 'The Mediterranean shipping amphoras from Arikamedu', in Begley & De Puma 1992: 151-6.

Will, E.L. 1996 'Mediterranean shipping amphoras at Arikamedu, 1941-50', in Begley et al. 1996: 317-49.

Will, E.L., 2004 'The Mediterranean shipping amphoras from 1990-92 excavations', in Begley et al. 2004: 325-403.

Williams, D.F. 2000 'Petrology of imported amphorae', in Phillipson 2000: 494-6.

Wolska-Conus, W. 1968-73 *Cosmas Indicopleustès, topographie chrétienne 1-3* (Sources chrétiennes 141, 159, Paris).

Young, G.K. 1997 'The customs-collector at the Nabataean port of Leuke Kome (*Periplus Maris Erythraei* 19)', *Zeitschrift für Papyrologie und Epigraphik* 119: 266-8.

Young, G.K. 2001 *Rome's Eastern Trade: International Commerce and Imperial Policy, 31 BC-AD 305* (London: Routledge).

Zemer, A. 1977 *Storage Jars in Ancient Sea Trade* (Haifa: The National Maritime Museum's Fund).

Ziethen, G. and Klingenberg, K. 2002 'Merchants, pilgrims and soliders on the Red Sea route', in P. Freeman, J. Bennett, Z.T. Fiema and B. Hoffmann (eds) *Limes XVIII: Proceedings of the XVIIIth International Congress of Roman Frontier Studies held in Amman, Jordon (September 2000)* (BAR Intl Ser. 1084(1), Oxford) 379-85.

Zvelebil, K. 1956 'The yavanas in old Tamil literature', *Charisteria Orientalia* (Praha: Československé akademie věd) 401-9.

Zvelebil, K. 1973 *The Smile of Murugan: On Tamil Literature of South India* (Leiden: E.J. Brill).

Zvelebil, K. 1974 *Tamil Literature* (Wiesbaden: Harrassowitz).

# Index

Numbers in bold refer to pages with figures.

*Index*

*Index*

oil, 28, 42, 74, 150; sesame and
ghee, 21, 75
Okelis, **12**, **101**, 102, 157
Omana, **12**, 109, **110**, 115, 116;
*see also* Ed Dur
Opone, **12**, 72, **94**, 96, 97, 99,
159; *see also* Ras Hafun
*ostraca*, 24-5, 58, 61, 74, 78,
81-2, 156-7; *see also* graffiti;
pottery, inscriptions on

Paithan, 118, **119**, 126, **127**, 130
Palghat, 33, 118, **119**, 144
Palmyra, **12**, 115, 154-5;
Palmyrenes, 80, 105, 108;
inscriptions, 79, 80, 84, 105;
religion, 62
Pandya, 37, 132-3, 138, 140-1,
171; coins, 145
Parthia/Parthians, as rivals
with Rome, 80, 114; finds,
39, 79, 96, 111, 122, 147;
influence, 125, 126
Pattanam, **12**, 47, 118, **119**, 126,
**127**, 132, 136, 142-3, 149,
156, 158-9, 161, 165, 167;
*see also* Muziris
pearls, 112, 139, 169-70
pepper, 16, 24, 55, 67, 76, 83,
138, 140, 141, 143, 155, 165,
170, 173, 174; *Horrea
piperataria*, 55; pepper pots,
55, 76, **77**, 174; sources of,
55
*Periplus Maris Erythraei* (*PME*),
20-2, 23, 29, 35, 42, 50, 54,
55, 57, 58, 61, 64, 65, 68, 69,
71, 72-3, 79, 88, 89, 90, 92,
94-5, 96, 97-8, 99, 100, 102,
103, 105, 106, 107-8, 109,

112, 114, 115, 116, 125-6,
129, 132, 135, 138, 140, 144,
148-9, 153, 158, 159, 160
Periyar River, 141
Persia/Persians, 18, 99, 101,
109, 120-1, 144, 145, 159,
160, 168, 170; finds, 42, 146
Petra, **59**, 68, 69, 155; *see also*
Nabataea
petrographic analysis, 38-9
Peutinger Table (*Tabula
Peutingeriana*), 30, 148
Pliny the Elder, 22, 29, 30-1,
54-5, 60, 63, 64, 81, 95, 140,
157
Poduke, **12**; *see also* Arikamedu
Pondicherry, *see* Arikamedu
pottery
Aksumite Coarse Wares, 52-4,
**53**, 77-8, 80, 81, 87, 104,
105, 107, 163; *see also*
pottery, East African
East African, Red Sandy
Ware, **53**, 53-4, 78, 80, 87;
*see also* pottery, Aksumite
Indian: Coarse Red-slipped
Wares (CRSW), 46-8, **47**,
50, 74-5, 87, 107, 142, 155;
Coarse Wares, 48, **49**, **75**,
75, **77**, 77, 87, 104, 161; *see
also* pepper, pepper pots;
Megalithic, 45-6, 75, 145,
147; mould decorated, 69,
155; Northern Black
Polished Ware (NBP), 44;
Organic Black Ware, 48, **49**,
50, 75, 87, 97, 107, 155-6,
161; Paddle Impressed
Wares, 48-50, **49**, 76, 87,
143; Red Polished Ware
(RPW), **45**, 46, 50, 107,

214